Managing Adverse and Reportable Information Regarding U.S. Military Officers

2019 Update

KATHERINE L. KIDDER, LAURA L. MILLER, SAMANTHA E. DINICOLA, PHILLIP CARTER

Prepared for the Office of the Secretary of Defense
Approved for public release; distribution unlimited

NATIONAL DEFENSE RESEARCH INSTITUTE

For more information on this publication, visit **www.rand.org/t/RRA126-1**.

About RAND

The RAND Corporation is a research organization that develops solutions to public policy challenges to help make communities throughout the world safer and more secure, healthier and more prosperous. RAND is nonprofit, nonpartisan, and committed to the public interest. To learn more about RAND, visit www.rand.org.

Research Integrity

Our mission to help improve policy and decisionmaking through research and analysis is enabled through our core values of quality and objectivity and our unwavering commitment to the highest level of integrity and ethical behavior. To help ensure our research and analysis are rigorous, objective, and nonpartisan, we subject our research publications to a robust and exacting quality-assurance process; avoid both the appearance and reality of financial and other conflicts of interest through staff training, project screening, and a policy of mandatory disclosure; and pursue transparency in our research engagements through our commitment to the open publication of our research findings and recommendations, disclosure of the source of funding of published research, and policies to ensure intellectual independence. For more information, visit www.rand.org/about/principles.

RAND's publications do not necessarily reflect the opinions of its research clients and sponsors.

Published by the RAND Corporation, Santa Monica, Calif.
© 2022 RAND Corporation
RAND® is a registered trademark.

Library of Congress Cataloging-in-Publication Data is available for this publication.
ISBN: 978-1-9774-0601-9

About This Report

The U.S. Constitution created roles for the President and Congress in the appointment of U.S. military officers. Title 10 of the U.S. Code sets forth the statutory rules that govern the process of appointing military officers, and the Senate Armed Services Committee (SASC) provides formal and informal guidance to the U.S. Department of Defense (DoD) regarding personnel actions requiring Senate confirmation.

In 2010, the RAND Corporation's National Defense Research Institute identified and reviewed DoD and military department policies and processes for managing substantiated adverse and other potentially unfavorable information to be considered in promotion, assignment, and retirement decisions regarding general and flag officers (G/FOs). That study revealed strengths and limitations in policies and processes and noted differences in DoD and SASC philosophies, with implications for what should be reported. A DoD working group reviewed that study's findings and recommendations, identified additional issues, and made specific recommendations that informed subsequent changes to policies and processes.

In 2019, DoD's Officer and Enlisted Personnel Management Office, General and Flag Officer Matters requested an updated assessment to document progress that had been made, new or persisting differences in how policies are interpreted, processes that differ by Service that might be problematic, and opportunities to correct any misalignment among Senate, Office of the Secretary of Defense (OSD), and Service expectations, policies, and processes. Additionally, the 2019 study scope was expanded to include adverse and reportable information policies and processes for promotions or appointments for commissioned officers in the pay grades below G/FOs and for officer transitions between Services or Service components.

OSD's goal is ensuring compliance with statutory intent based on congressional guidance and instilling the highest possible confidence in the reliability of information provided to the Secretary of Defense, the secretaries of the military departments, and members of the officer promotion selection boards. This report on the 2019 review might be of interest to military officers, personnel involved in military officer personnel actions, and decisionmakers. The research reported here was completed in August 2020 and underwent security review with the sponsor and the Defense Office of Prepublication and Security Review before public release.

RAND National Security Research Division

This research was sponsored by the Office of the Deputy Assistant Secretary of Defense (Military Personnel Policy) and conducted within the Forces and Resources Policy Center of the RAND National Security Research Division (NSRD), which operates the National Defense Research Institute (NDRI), a federally funded research and development center sponsored by the Office of the Secretary of Defense, the Joint Staff, the Unified Combatant Commands, the Navy, the Marine Corps, the defense agencies, and the defense intelligence enterprise.

For more information on the RAND Forces and Resources Policy Center, see www.rand.org/nsrd/frp or contact the director (contact information is provided on the webpage).

Contents

Figures and Tables

Summary

The U.S. President has the power, by and with the advice and consent of the U.S. Senate, to appoint officers of the United States. Military officer appointments, promotions, and retirements are governed by formal and informal statute, policy, and guidance. Requirements seek to ensure that officers—especially senior officers—demonstrate the exemplary conduct necessary for the authority and responsibilities they hold. For example, Title 10 of the U.S. Code requires consideration of adverse information by all boards considering active officers for promotion to the pay grade of O-4 and above and reserve officers for promotion to the pay grade of O-6 and above, including general and flag officer (G/FO) promotion boards. The process of identifying, conveying, and reviewing adverse and other reportable information regarding these officers involves interactions between the military department secretaries, the Office of the Secretary of Defense (OSD), the White House, and, through the Senate Armed Services Committee (SASC), the Senate.

In 2010, the RAND Corporation's National Defense Research Institute conducted a study sponsored by the Under Secretary of Defense for Personnel and Readiness (USD[P&R]) that described and evaluated reporting processes of the Services and the U.S. Department of Defense (DoD) for G/FOs. This study update is intended to describe any recent progress made in reporting processes, identify any new or remaining issues, and make recommendations for any improvements to policy or processes that are needed to help ensure that consistent, reliable information supports decisions regarding the promotion and appointment of military officers.

Study Approach

We gathered and reviewed DoD and Service policies, memos, guidance, relevant sections of Title 10 of the U.S. Code, and other documents related to the identification, recording, or reporting of adverse and reportable information for military officers. We also met with representatives from the DoD and Service offices involved in these processes and with SASC staff who assist SASC members in assessing military officer personnel action packages, or files.

Key Findings

Policy Definitions and Reporting Requirements

The updated 2014 policy offers more detail and clarity on definitions and reporting requirements than the previous policy, but some ambiguity remains. For example, it is unclear whether the Services should be conducting internet searches to identify officers connected with significant events widely known to the general public that meet the reportable information threshold, and, if so, what search criteria are expected. Furthermore, the policy is not explicit on whether the definition of adverse information intentionally excludes information with a probable cause determination, a lower threshold of proof than the preponderance of the evidence standard. Also, there is variation in Service understandings of the phrase "investigation or inquiry," with some offices delineating an "intake" or "pre-investigation" phase, in which a complaint has been received but the office is verifying elements of the allegation (e.g., which individual is being accused) and deciding whether to open a formal investigation. Trust with the Senate can be eroded when members learn after a vote that the Services were aware of an open allegation against an officer but did not report it in time for the members' consideration.

The definition of *adverse* in DoD Instruction (DoDI) 1320.04 permits the exclusion of incidents that have resulted in no more than nonpunitive rehabilitative counseling.[1] Different superior officers may choose different courses of action in response to the same behavior. Thus, the language in the definition introduces opportunities for inconsistent reporting of adverse information across officers and across Services, because the policy permits behaviors to be reported as adverse for some officers but not for others on the basis of the type of action their superiors took.

DoDI 1320.04 also does not define the adverse and reportable information process for officers seeking cross-Service or cross-component transfers.

Personnel Processes

The processes for identifying, reviewing, and reporting adverse and reportable information are labor-intensive and time-consuming and require coordination across many offices. The updated 2014 policy outlining personnel action processes built upon and expanded the previous 1995 DoDI in multiple ways, integrating guidance previously published in several subsequent memoranda, such as those regarding G/FO retirements; expanding and clearly documenting Service, military department, and Joint Chiefs of Staff responsibilities for ensuring policy compliance; and explicitly listing the records the Services must check for adverse and reportable information for pay grades of O-7 and above. Good working relationships across many organizations help staff with judgment calls in complicated situations, questions about policy application, and status updates as the personnel action packages move through the process.

Recent developments include the fiscal year (FY) 2019 National Defense Authorization Act (NDAA) authorizing officers who have open investigations of misconduct to conditionally retire, which provides the option to revisit the retirement pay grade determination upon the conclusion of the investigation. Thus, in cases in which it appears highly unlikely that allegations against the retiring officers will be substantiated, the officers and their families can be permitted to move forward and to access retirement benefits rather than waiting months or even years for the investigation to conclude. More recently, the FY 2020 NDAA amended Title 10 of the U.S. Code[2] to mandate that adverse information now be furnished to additional promotion selection boards (boards considering promotion to O-4 and above for active-component officers and to O-6 and above for reserve-component officers rather than just

[1] DoDI 1320.04, *Military Officer Actions Requiring Presidential, Secretary of Defense, or Under Secretary of Defense for Personnel and Readiness Approval or Senate Confirmation*, Washington, D.C.: U.S. Department of Defense, January 3, 2014.

[2] 10 U.S.C. 615(a)(3).

boards considering promotion to G/FO ranks). The Services report that allocated resources are inadequate to manage the significantly increased workload.

Sources of Adverse and Reportable Information

Potential sources of adverse and reportable information are located within and outside DoD. Sources that must be checked for G/FO personnel actions are now listed in DoDI 1320.04. Among those explicitly named are the Military Equal Opportunity (MEO) and Equal Employment Opportunity (EEO) program files, which the 2010 RAND assessment had found were not both being consistently checked, because some staff were not aware of the distinction.[3] One policy compliance challenge is that the Federal Bureau of Investigation's (FBI's) National Crime Information Center (NCIC) database cannot be checked as required by DoD policy, because authorization is limited to only law enforcement agencies for law enforcement purposes.

Service offices have benefited from upgrades to their systems for checking sources for adverse and reportable information. However, some database and workforce limitations present significant and persistent obstacles to moving these packages through the processes in a timely manner. The expanded scope required by the FY 2020 NDAA to provide data checks on even more and significantly larger groups of officers increases these workforce demands. Without improvements to such data systems, the Services will have an increased demand on the workforce to meet the new requirement, or the thoroughness of the data checks might be compromised, or there could be a backlog in conducting these checks that keeps some officers' records from being completed on time. Delays in checking data sources and completing investigations can create more opportunities or incentives for valued officers to leave military service rather than wait for the delayed promotion or assignment decisions. Delays can also result in gaps in filling leadership positions or some positions being filled by less qualified officers. Additionally, drawn-out, unresolved investigations of allegations against officers can undermine their reputations and authority and cause potentially lasting damage, even for officers who are ultimately exonerated.

Even though many databases are checked for adverse or reportable information, some databases, such as professional license investigation records or the employee records of National Guard and reserve officers who are also DoD civilian employees, are not explicitly required to be checked.

The Service headquarters have differing levels of access to unfavorable information found in command-directed investigations (CDIs); as a result, that information is not consistently reported in officer personnel action packages. Headquarters-level Service process requirements range from tracking all CDIs into officers as soon as they are opened (Air Force and Marine Corps), to tracking only substantiated adverse findings for officers O-4 and above after the investigations are completed (Army), to having no centralized tracking of CDIs at all (Navy). These differences put some officers who were investigated by their commander at a career disadvantage compared with their peers in other Services. Services lacking a centralized database with complete CDI information risk clearing a nominee who might in fact have adverse or reportable information that will come to light at a later point in the confirmation process.

---

3 MEO files track complaints by military personnel, while EEO files track complaints by civilian employees.

U.S. Department of Defense and Senate Armed Services Committee Practices and Perspectives

The Services and DoD will never review officer files with the exact same lens as the SASC. The additional information required in DoDI 1320.04 better aligns DoD policy and practice with SASC expectations. However, different perspectives and approaches to managing adverse and reportable information still exist and can be the source of SASC dissatisfaction with certain personnel action packages it receives and, in turn, some Service or DoD surprise at SASC requests or actions. SASC staff emphasize that senators evaluate adverse and reportable information in personnel packages according to not only whether allegations of officers violating rules or laws were substantiated but also whether the officers displayed integrity, good leadership, and sound judgment. Thus, investigation information from unsubstantiated allegations might be requested in such cases. Additionally, the SASC expects the adverse and reportable information summaries to be neutral and factual, reflect all adverse and reportable information, and demonstrate that the military department secretaries and Service Chiefs were provided with an accurate sense of the officers they are endorsing for appointment, promotion, or assignment. The military department secretary's separate memorandum is where leadership can make a persuasive argument that the officer meets the exemplary conduct standards despite the adverse information.

Where to draw the line on what information to report is a source of ongoing concern. Currently, there is no established list of information that the SASC thinks should be reported, although some of its interests, such as any association with any unit being investigated for detainee abuse, are well known through experience. The SASC staff prefers that the Services err on the side of providing more-complete information. Also, in some exceptional cases, the SASC will request information beyond the ten-year time frame stipulated in policy.

SASC staff noted that officers have expressed and occasionally have acted on fears that the presence of any adverse or reportable information in a nomination package will automatically disqualify an officer from confirmation; however, that is not the case. Senators want to be aware of and understand the circumstances under which an incident or complaint might arise so that they can make informed decisions and address questions that might arise from their constituents. It is also critical that commanders do not fail to take appropriate action with subordinates or document unfavorable information as required because of assumptions that doing so would eliminate the possibility for those subordinates to advance to and within the senior level.

For Further Study

Additional common themes raised during this 2019 study merit consideration for further study. In particular, we heard repeated concerns that complaints against officers were being "weaponized," or reported at strategic moments simply to derail officers' careers. Further study would be needed to understand the nature, extent, or impact of such a phenomenon, if it does indeed exist. Additionally, the full impact of the timeline necessary to process personnel packages containing adverse or reportable information—including the impact on individual officers, their authority and ability to lead while facing open allegations, their career opportunities, and their motivation to remain in the military—is not well documented. Moreover, it would be valuable to explore the impact of drawn-out officer investigations on their units' morale and cohesion and the risk to subordinates when the officers who have indeed engaged in misconduct remain in positions of authority until the investigation is closed.

Recommendations

We make several recommendations for OSD and the Services to consider to clarify the processes for using adverse and reportable information regarding military officer appointments, assignments, promotions, and retirements. Some recommendations are less specific than others because the DoD Adverse and Reportable Information Working Group will be convening to deliberate details necessary for any changes to be adopted. More details about these recommendations are provided in Chapter Seven of this report.

Policy Definitions and Reporting Requirements

Recommendations regarding policy definitions and reporting requirements are as follows:

- OSD should further refine the adverse and reportable information definitions and reporting requirements to address ambiguities in DoDI 1320.04 and to align DoD and Senate requirements. For example, the policy should clarify whether the probable-cause standard meets the adverse information threshold, that the SASC does not recognize a "pre-investigation" phase following a complaint, and whether internet searches for unfavorable information are expected.
- OSD should remove from the adverse information criteria the language stating that the level or type of a superior's disciplinary action in response to an officer's behavior should in part determine whether substantiated allegations should be reported.

Personnel Processes

Recommendations regarding personnel processes are as follows:

- OSD and the Services should sustain and extend the positive aspects of current processes, such as modernizing data systems, maintaining good relationships and communication across organizations, and maintaining data-safeguarding measures to prevent leaks and maintain the integrity of the process.
- OSD should detail in policy the adverse and reportable information reporting requirements and processes for officers seeking cross-Service and cross-component transfers.

Sources of Adverse and Reportable Information

Recommendations regarding sources of adverse and reportable information are as follows:

- OSD and the Services should invest in data systems and personnel dedicated to these processes to ensure that the data checks are as complete and accurate as possible and that the packages proceed in an efficient and timely manner.
- OSD should require changes to remedy the lack of standardization among the Services regarding headquarters-level access to information from CDIs and monitor for compliance.
- OSD should update DoDI 1320.04 to remove the required check of the FBI's NCIC database for G/FO personnel actions, since it is not an authorized use of this database, and indicate any replacement.
- OSD should consider whether additional data sources—such as professional license or privilege investigation records or the civilian employee records for National Guard and

reserve officers who are also DoD civilian employees—can and should be checked for adverse or reportable information.

- The Services should prepare a user-friendly officer's guide on adverse and reportable information definitions, reporting requirements, and procedures to promote compliance with Service and DoD requirements.

U.S. Department of Defense and Senate Armed Services Committee Practices and Perspectives

Recommendations regarding DoD and SASC practices and perspectives are as follows:

- The General and Flag Officer Matters Office (G/FO Matters) should discuss with the DoD and Service inspector general (IG) offices potential options to address IG concerns about requirements to include unredacted investigation files in personnel action packages for the SASC. If an alternative is feasible and the SASC approves, G/FO Matters should formalize any new requirements through policy.
- OSD and the Services should provide guidance and training to the responsible individuals on how to prepare neutral, factual, and complete adverse and reportable information summaries that meet SASC expectations.

Acknowledgments

We appreciate the dedicated project support and guidance provided by Deputy Director Cheryl Black and Chief Warrant Officer 3 Donald R. Crutchfield of G/FO Matters, Office of the Deputy Assistant Secretary of Defense (Military Personnel Policy).

This research could not have been accomplished without the cooperation of representatives from numerous offices in OSD and the Services involved in identifying, recording, and reporting adverse and reportable information regarding military officers. The information and insights that they provided were essential to understanding existing policies and processes and where improvements could be beneficial. Representatives who met with us include

- Anthony Jones, Jeff Morris, Charles St. Cyr, and Patrick Gookin (DoD Office of the Inspector General)
- Christopher Brown (Defense Human Resources Activity)
- Steven Strong (OSD, Office of the General Counsel)
- Michael Melillo, Dale Bourque, Lindsay Reiner, and MAJ Judy Carbonell (OEPM)
- COL Lisa Griffin, Arthur Stovall, Jean Romero, and COL Patrick Altenburg (Joint Staff)
- Brig Gen Michael Gerock, John Ellington, and COL William Greer (National Guard Bureau)
- David Dillensnyder, Mark Vandervort, LCDR Shelley Branch, LtCol Jennifer Parker, CDR Luke Whittemore, Thomas Miller, CDR Amanda Myers, Steven Milewski, Kristinn Coleman, CAPT Christopher Williams, LCDR Adam Yost, Cheryl Miller, Celina Kline, Mary Horrigan, CAPT Joshua Nauman, CDR Tanya Cruz, CAPT Vincent Smith, LT Mark Wilson, and LT Michael Watrol (Navy offices)
- BG Thomas Edwards, Leah Reid, CPT Jessica Lucas, Heidi Hanley, COL John Jurden, LTC Eric Noble, Amy Luyster, Shahara (Tennaile) Timbrook, COL Timothy Holman, COL Sula Irish, Albert Eggerton, LTC Brett Medlin, Henry Finley, COL Mark Sydenham, Barry Hadley, Spurgeon Moore, Tish Ash, Kimberly Loder-Albritton, and LTC Michael Johnson (Army offices)
- Col Brian Hinsvark, Matthew Bartlett, Bradley Arnold, Matthew Williams, Thomas Jaster, Ralph (Brian) Arnold, Margarete Ashmore, Col Tiffany Dawson, Col Colin Connor, Margaret Sweizer, Jamie (Scott) Brady, Lt Col Matthew Huibregste, Maj Ruth Afiesimama, Col Sarah Mangahas, Rita Looney, Carol Hamilton, Mary Morfitt, and Capt Kristen Baker (Air Force offices)
- Col Kristin McCann, Robert Cheshire, LtCol Geoffrey Shows, Capt Michael Minerva, David Edson, Maj Tanzania Jaysura, and Peter Ferraro (Marine Corps offices).

Additionally, meetings with SASC professional staff members provided important perspectives on SASC priorities and concerns and the processes involved in reviewing military officer personnel packages for actions that require Senate confirmation. We thank Gary Leeling, Jonathan Clarke, Stephanie Barna, and Leah Brewer.

Lisa Harrington and Craig Bond at RAND provided feedback on project briefings and an initial draft of this report, which helped inform this document. We also thank communications analyst Melissa Bauman for assistance in creating process figures and reviewing portions of an earlier draft of this report. William Chambers and Lisa Harrington served as our quality assurance peer reviewers, and we are grateful for their expert insights and thoughtful comments. Finally, we thank Emily Ward for her thorough and thoughtful copyediting.

Abbreviations

AFI	Air Force Instruction
AR	Army Regulation
CAF	Consolidated Adjudication Facility
CDI	command-directed investigation
CJCS	chairman of the Joint Chiefs of Staff
CJCSI	Chairman of the Joint Chiefs of Staff Instruction
DA	Department of the Army
DoD	U.S. Department of Defense
DoDD	Department of Defense Directive
DoDI	Department of Defense Instruction
EEO	Equal Employment Opportunity
EEOC	U.S. Equal Employment Opportunity Commission
EO	equal opportunity
FBI	Federal Bureau of Investigation
FY	fiscal year
GC	general counsel
GDMA	Glenn-Defense Marine Asia
G/FO	general and flag officer
G/FO Matters	General and Flag Officer Matters Office
HASC	House Armed Services Committee
IG	inspector general
IRCMS	Investigations and Resolutions Case Management System
IRD	Investigations and Resolution Directorate

JA	judge advocate
JAG	judge advocate general
JAGINST	JAG Instruction
JAGMAN	Manual of the Judge Advocate General
MCO	Marine Corps Order
MEO	Military Equal Opportunity
NCIC	National Crime Information Center
NDAA	National Defense Authorization Act
NGI	Next Generation Identification
NJP	nonjudicial punishment
ODN	Officer Disciplinary Notebook
OEPM	Officer and Enlisted Personnel Management Office
OIG	Office of the Inspector General
OSD	Office of the Secretary of Defense
OUSD(P&R)	Office of the Under Secretary of Defense for Personnel and Readiness
PDUSD(P&R)	Principal Deputy Under Secretary of Defense for Personnel and Readiness
RMO	responsible management official
SASC	Senate Armed Services Committee
SJA	staff judge advocate
UCMJ	Uniform Code of Military Justice
USD(P&R)	Under Secretary of Defense for Personnel and Readiness

CHAPTER ONE

Introduction

In this report, we describe and evaluate U.S. Department of Defense (DoD) and Service policies and processes for tracking and reporting substantiated adverse and other potentially unfavorable information about military officers to be considered in personnel actions, such as promotions, assignments, and retirements. Sponsored by the Office of the Deputy Assistant Secretary of Defense (Military Personnel Policy), this research updates and expands the scope of a RAND National Defense Research Institute evaluation examining the management of adverse and other reportable information regarding general and flag officers (G/FOs) that was conducted in 2010 and published in 2012.[1] That research revealed strengths and shortcomings in policies and processes, gaps in understanding among those involved in the process, and differing DoD and Senate Armed Services Committee (SASC) philosophies that sometimes led to different conclusions about what should be reported. The 2010 review also offered several recommendations to address the identified issues.

There are several rationales for a reassessment. DoD and Service policies and processes regarding adverse and reportable information have changed since the 2010 research was completed. There have been numerous high-profile cases of misconduct among U.S. senior military officers that continue to draw attention to how such cases are handled. SASC professional staff have recommended that DoD review current processes to ensure that they continue to meet statutory requirements. Additionally, DoD is preparing to update the primary policy on adverse and reportable information and would like to address any ambiguities or critical gaps as it does so.[2] The consequences of DoD lacking timely access to adverse and reportable information are significant and might result in faulty decisions, loss of credibility with Congress, and loss of public confidence in DoD. This report describes recent progress made in reporting processes, identifies new and remaining issues, and recommends improvements to policy or processes to help ensure that consistent, reliable information supports personnel decisions regarding U.S. military officers.

---

[1] Margaret C. Harrell and William M. Hix, *Managing Adverse and Reportable Information Regarding General and Flag Officers*, Santa Monica, Calif.: RAND Corporation, MG-1088-OSD, 2012.

[2] DoD Instruction (DoDI) 1320.04, *Military Officer Actions Requiring Presidential, Secretary of Defense, or Under Secretary of Defense for Personnel and Readiness Approval or Senate Confirmation*, Washington, D.C.: U.S. Department of Defense, January 3, 2014.

Research Questions and Scope

This research focused exclusively on adverse and reportable information regarding U.S. commissioned military officers—not warrant officers or enlisted personnel. The management of DoD civilian personnel was outside the scope of this research.[3] The research effort was guided by the following questions:

1. What changes have been made to DoD and Service policies and processes for managing adverse and reportable information regarding G/FOs since the 2010 RAND Corporation review?
2. What are the policies and processes for managing adverse and reportable information regarding officers in pay grades O-6 and below?
3. To what extent are there new or persisting issues regarding the interpretation or application of policies on adverse and reportable information?
4. What can be done to address any misalignment between Senate, DoD, and Service expectations, policies, and processes?

Adverse and reportable information policies and processes related to the following personnel actions fell within the scope of our study:

- reporting requirements for promotions or appointments for officers in pay grades O-6 and below
- officer transitions between Services (e.g., Army to Air Force)
- officer transitions among active, National Guard, and reserve components
- G/FO appointments, promotions, and retirements.

As later chapters will reveal, personnel actions for G/FOs (O-7 to O-10) are managed differently than they are for officers in pay grades O-6 and below.

Research Approach

This research is based on several complementary sources of information. These include

- previous RAND research on the management of adverse and other reportable information regarding G/FOs and available versions of the DoD and Service policies and guidance cited in it[4]
- relevant current DoD and Service policy, memos, and guidance
- relevant sections of Title 10 of the U.S. Code
- meetings with DoD and Service representatives who manage these processes or are involved in recording or checking adverse information, including
  – G/FO management offices

---

[3]   Some reserve officers are also DoD civilian employees, and a subset of these are *military technicians* whose employment terms differ from those of their civilian employee or reserve officer counterparts (see 10 U.S.C. 10216 for further details). Only the management of the military role of reserve officers falls within the scope of our study.

[4]   The previous RAND research is Harrell and Hix, 2012.

- management offices for officers in pay grades O-6 and below
- inspectors general (IGs)
- Equal Employment Opportunity (EEO) and Military Equal Opportunity (MEO) program offices
- judge advocates (JAs) and general counsels (GCs)
- the Joint Staff
- the National Guard Bureau
- discussions with experts on the Federal Bureau of Investigation's (FBI's) National Crime Information Center (NCIC) database
- meetings with SASC professional staff, as well as recent legislation and public statements by members of Congress regarding the monitoring or reporting of adverse information.

Our approach to each meeting was guided by our research questions but tailored to the particular representatives in attendance. Broadly, the main topics we asked about during the meetings included

- representatives' tenures and roles in the office
- the office's role in managing adverse and reportable information in the personnel processes
- the scope of the office's role (e.g., pay grades, types of adverse or reportable information)
- other offices that the office interacts with during these personnel processes
- specific policies that the office uses to guide this work
- characteristics and usage of any databases or tools
- changes to policies or processes since 2010
- how the office interprets and applies policies on adverse and reportable information, including any cases that revealed policy ambiguities that required some discussion or coordination to resolve
- any changes to relevant policies or processes that are planned or underway
- any new or persistent problems and potential solutions.

We sorted documents and meeting notes by organization—for example, Navy, National Guard Bureau, DoD Under Secretary of Defense for Personnel and Readiness (USD[P&R]), and Congress. For each of the four Services at the time (Army, Navy, Air Force, and Marine Corps),[5] one of us took the lead on gathering and understanding the Service's policies and processes, which included the policies and processes for the corresponding military departments (Army, Navy, Air Force). The research questions mentioned earlier guided our information gathering, review, and analysis.

Note that we did not directly examine the personnel action files for military officers, nor did we directly observe the processes described by interviewees or outlined in the policy documents or guides. Moreover, meetings with SASC staff and reviews of legislation and congressional statements provided context for this project's research focus on the Office of the Secretary of Defense (OSD) and the Services. It was not within the scope of our project to study and make recommendations about SASC policies and processes.

---

[5]   The U.S. Space Force was established on December 20, 2019, when the project was approaching completion, so it could not be included in this project.

Key Terms

Later in this report, we review in detail the policy definitions of adverse and reportable information. However, several other relevant terms used in this report are also important to understand:

- **Promotion selection board:** a board of commissioned officers convened by the secretary of a military department to evaluate and recommend qualified officers for promotion to a higher pay grade.[6]
- **Special selection board:** a board convened by the secretary of a military department to evaluate the record of an officer who was not considered by a promotion board because of administrative error or who was considered by a promotion board in what was deemed an unfair manner. The special selection board makes a promotion recommendation based on a review of the officer's record, a sample of records of officers in the same competitive category who were recommended for promotion by that board, and a sample of officers who were not recommended for promotion by that same board.[7]
- **Federal recognition board:** a board of commissioned officers designated by the Secretary of the Army (for the Army National Guard) or the Secretary of the Air Force (for the Air National Guard) to evaluate whether an officer's original appointment or promotion to a higher pay grade in the state's National Guard is eligible for federal recognition. If the federal recognition board determines that the officer is qualified, the Chief of the National Guard Bureau may issue a certificate of eligibility, applicable for two years, that entitles that individual to fill a vacancy in the National Guard for either an original appointment or a position that would require a promotion to a higher pay grade.[8]
- **Promotion review board:** a board convened by the secretary of a military department to review adverse information before a recommendation for nomination is submitted to the Secretary of Defense in cases in which the adverse information had not been reviewed by the promotion selection board, special selection board, or federal recognition board.
- **Package(s):** in this context, the collected set of necessary documents assembled in support of a personnel action, such as an appointment, a promotion, or a retirement.
- **Personnel actions:** the personnel actions that are the focus of this report are officer appointments, promotions, and retirements. An *original appointment* is the initial action accessing an officer through a military commission, but it also applies to other active- or reserve-component transitions and transfers that are neither promotions nor demotions. The term *appointment* applies to senior officers, too; a G/FO can be nominated for appointment to a position established by statute, such as a combatant commander, Service Chief, or commandant. More broadly, a *promotion* is an advancement in military rank and pay grade. Military officers become eligible for *retirement* after 20 years of qualifying service or a qualifying medical disability.[9]

---

[6]   U.S. law establishes requirements for the composition and processes of these boards (10 U.S.C., Chapters 36 and 1403).

[7]   10 U.S.C. 628; 10 U.S.C. 14502.

[8]   32 U.S.C. 307.

[9]   For more information, see Kristy N. Kamarck, *Military Retirement: Background and Recent Developments*, Washington, D.C.: Congressional Research Service, RL34751, last updated July 12, 2019.

- **Personnel action processes:** the means by which personnel actions are formalized. Officers can be *selected* for promotion by a promotion selection board, position vacancy board, or special selection board. The military department secretaries review those selections and *recommend* officers for promotion. The military department secretaries can also recommend that officers be nominated for appointment to assignments in the pay grades of O-9 and O-10. The Secretary of Defense can *approve* the recommendations of the military department secretaries. Officers are considered *nominated* for a promotion or assignment when the President approves their nomination. Promotions and assignments are *confirmed* by the Senate. *Federal recognition* is a process specific to the National Guard in which the state promotes an officer to fill a vacancy, but the promotion must be federally recognized. Upon being federally recognized, officers in the grades of O-1 to O-5 are appointed by the Secretary of Defense, while officers in the grades of O-6 and above are appointed by the President with the advice and consent of the Senate.[10]

Organization of This Report

Chapter Two provides background and context for this evaluation, including the legal bases for military officer appointment and confirmation, an overview of the results from RAND's 2010 review of adverse and reportable information reporting,[11] and DoD's rationale for this research update.

Chapter Three reviews the current DoD policy definitions of adverse and reportable information, describes how they improved upon the previous policy definitions, and documents ambiguities reported by the offices responsible for applying these policies at the Service or DoD level.

Chapter Four explains the Service and DoD processes through which adverse and reportable information is gathered, assessed, reported, and reviewed for military officers undergoing various personnel actions, including how those processes vary by pay grade, what important changes have been made since RAND's 2010 review, and new or persisting gaps or inconsistencies.

Chapter Five addresses the different sources of adverse and reportable information, what types of information they contain, how and when the Services check these sources and challenges in doing so, relevant Service consistencies and differences in these sources, and other potential sources of adverse and reportable information that were not being checked at the time of this study.

Chapter Six highlights SASC reviews of military officer personnel packages, expectations regarding the inclusion of adverse and reportable information, and concerns relevant for DoD and Service policies and processes.

Chapter Seven summarizes the research findings and offers recommendations for consideration as OSD and the Services look to refine and update their policies and processes.

---

[10]   10 U.S.C. 12203(a); 10 U.S.C. 12211; 10 U.S.C. 12212.

[11]   Harrell and Hix, 2012.

Appendix A lists the key policies consulted in the course of this project. Appendix B presents the unedited DoD templates for adverse and reportable information summaries that are included in officer personnel packages.

CHAPTER TWO

Background and Context

This chapter introduces the legal bases for the appointment and confirmation of military officers. These include the requirement that those officers have demonstrated exemplary conduct and the primary DoD policy instructing how the legal requirements will be met. This chapter also provides a brief overview of previous research on DoD and Service policies and processes assessing the conduct of G/FOs and the rationale for the expanded and updated research described in this report.

Legal Bases for Appointment and Confirmation of Officers

Three clauses of the U.S. Constitution provide the bases for the appointment or commission of "officers of the United States," and, in certain cases, their confirmation by the Senate. The most significant is the Appointments Clause of the Constitution, which empowers the President to nominate officers, subject to the advice and consent of the Senate.[1] This constitutional clause reads:

> He shall have Power, by and with the Advice and Consent of the Senate, to make Treaties, provided two thirds of the Senators present concur; and *he shall nominate, and by and with the Advice and Consent of the Senate*, shall appoint Ambassadors, other public Ministers and Consuls, Judges of the supreme Court, and *all other Officers of the United States*, whose Appointments are not herein otherwise provided for, and which shall be established by Law: but the Congress may by Law vest the appointment of such inferior Officers, as they think proper, in the President alone, in the Courts of Law, or in the Heads of Departments.[2]

---

[1] The Appointments Clause was modeled on a provision in the Massachusetts Constitution that made its way into the U.S. Constitution via an amendment sponsored by New Hampshire delegate Nathaniel Gorham. See Harvard Law School, "Congressional Restrictions on the President's Appointment Power and the Role of Longstanding Practice in Constitutional Interpretation," *Harvard Law Review*, Vol. 120, No. 7, May 2007, which cites James Madison, *The Debates in the Federal Convention of 1787 Which Framed the Constitution of the United States of America*, eds. Gaillard Hunt and James Brown Scott, New York: Oxford University Press, [1787] 1920. It is unclear why the Constitutional Convention preferred the Senate to the House of Representatives for this advice and consent role, although the Senate's historical overview of the nominations process suggests that it was chosen to protect the rights of small states in the appointments process and ensure that Presidential appointees did not favor large states. U.S. Senate, "Nominations: A Historical Overview," webpage, undated.

[2] U.S. Constitution, Article II, Section 2, Philadelphia, Pa., 1788, emphasis added.

Article II, Section 3 further states that the President "shall Commission all the Officers of the United States."[3] In addition to these clauses in Article II (the article describing the Executive Branch), Article I, Section 8 of the Constitution vests in Congress the powers to "raise and support Armies . . . [t]o provide and maintain a Navy," and to "make Rules for the Government and Regulation of the land and naval Forces."[4]

In some of its earliest acts after the Constitution's ratification, the first Congress established precedent for how these clauses would intersect with executive authority and military force structure.[5] Commissioned officers were all to be nominated by the President, with the advice and consent of the Senate; noncommissioned officers did not go through such a confirmation process. This early legislation governing the military established a practice that diverged from practice at civilian agencies, where only the cabinet secretary or other senior officials were considered "officers of the United States" subject to confirmation by the Senate. This legal distinction between military officers and civilian "officers" might reflect both the additional role for Congress under Article I, Section 8 in making rules for the military and common understanding at the time the Constitution was drafted and ratified.[6] In recent cases, the Supreme Court has declared that "the Appointments Clause applies to military officers,"[7] while distinguishing the appointment and commissioning powers (which required Senate confirmation) from the "power to 'assign' officers" to positions or commands.[8]

During the modern era, Congress has continued its practice of legislating requirements for the promotion of officers. For example, federal law now describes the legal requirements for convening, composition, notice, confidentiality, and operation of promotion boards, as well as the legal procedures for handling their recommendations and reports and requiring confirmation by the Senate (e.g., for active-component officers at or above the grade of O-4).[9] For active officers, Title 10 of the U.S. Code confers the authority on the "President alone" for "original appointments" in the grades of O-1, O-2, and O-3 but states that "original appointments" in the grades of O-4, O-5, and O-6 "shall be made by the President, by and with the advice and consent of the Senate."[10] In a case in which the Senate does not give its advice and consent to the appointment of an officer submitted for confirmation, or does not do so in a timely manner, federal law requires removing the officer's name from the promotion list.[11] Consideration of the conduct of officers extends to retirement as well, requiring that officers

---

[3]   U.S. Constitution, Article II, Section 3, Philadelphia, Pa., 1788.

[4]   U.S. Constitution, Article I, Section 8, Philadelphia, Pa., 1788.

[5]   See U.S. Statutes at Large, 1st Congress, 2nd session, Statute II, Chapter 9, An Act for the Punishment of Certain Crimes Against the United States, April 30, 1790.

[6]   Jennifer L. Mascott, "Who Are 'Officers of the United States'?" *Stanford Law Review*, Vol. 70, No. 2, February 2018, pp. 443, 481–483, 529–531.

[7]   *Weiss v. United States*, 510 U.S. 163 (1994) (rejected Appointments Clause challenge to the membership of the Court of Military Appeals because, among other things, the judges were appointed by the President and confirmed by the Senate as military officers).

[8]   *Edmond v. United States*, 520 U.S. 651, 657–658 (1997) (rejected Appointments Clause challenge to the authority of the Coast Guard Court of Criminal Appeals).

[9]   10 U.S.C. 611–618.

[10]   10 U.S.C. 531.

[11]   10 U.S.C. 629.

retire in the highest grade they held satisfactorily and allowing the secretaries of the military departments to consider findings of misconduct to decide whether to retire officers at their highest grade or a lesser one.[12]

The statutes governing officer promotion require "exemplary conduct" on the part of officers being considered for appointment and confirmation, defining such conduct as "show[ing] in themselves a good example of virtue, honor, patriotism, and subordination" and "to guard against and suppress all dissolute and immoral practices, and to correct, according to the laws and regulations of the . . . [Army, Navy, or Air Force], all persons who are guilty of them."[13] To ensure that officers meet this standard, the federal statute governing officer promotions empowers the Secretary of Defense to delay the appointments of officers if

(A) sworn charges against the officer have been received by an officer exercising general court-martial jurisdiction over the officer and such charges have not been disposed of;
(B) an investigation is being conducted to determine whether disciplinary action of any kind should be brought against the officer;
(C) a board of officers has been convened under chapter 60 of this title to review the record of the officer; or
(D) a criminal proceeding in a Federal or State court is pending against the officer.[14]

Additionally, for reserve officers, 10 U.S.C. 14311 includes a fifth condition: the Secretary of Defense can delay the officer's appointment if "substantiated adverse information about the officer that is material to the decision to appoint the officer is under review by the Secretary of Defense or the Secretary concerned."

This rule is further operationalized by the federal statute governing information provided to selection boards, which directs the Secretary of Defense to prescribe regulations governing what information—adverse or otherwise—may be considered by selection boards.[15] As written at the time of this research (mid-2019), federal law required that "any credible information of an adverse nature, including any substantiated adverse finding or conclusion from an officially documented investigation or inquiry, shall be furnished to the selection board" for officers being considered for promotion to O-7 or above.[16] Under these statutes, officers whose files will contain adverse information are required to have such information made available to them prior to the board and to have a "reasonable opportunity to submit comments on that infor-

---

[12]   10 U.S.C. 1370.

[13]   Title 10 provides three Service-specific references to the requirement for exemplary conduct: Section 7233 (Army), Section 8167 (Navy and Marine Corps), and Section 9233 (Air Force). The statute defines *exemplary conduct* in four parts, requiring all "commanding officers and others in authority" in a Service

(1) to show in themselves a good example of virtue, honor, patriotism, and subordination;
(2) to be vigilant in inspecting the conduct of all persons who are placed under their command;
(3) to guard against and suppress all dissolute and immoral practices, and to correct, according to the laws and regulations of the . . . [Service], all persons who are guilty of them; and
(4) to take all necessary and proper measures, under the laws, regulations, and customs of the . . . [Service], to promote and safeguard the morale, the physical well-being, and the general welfare of the officers and enlisted persons under their command or charge.

[14]   10 U.S.C. 624. Note that this statute is mirrored in 10 U.S.C. 14311, which applies to reserve officers.

[15]   10 U.S.C. 615; 10 U.S.C. 14107.

[16]   10 U.S.C. 615; 10 U.S.C. 14107.

mation to the selection board."[17] Selection boards are then directed by statute to recommend officers for promotion only when "a majority of the members of the board, after consideration by all members of the board of any adverse information about the officer . . . finds that the officer is among the officers best qualified for promotion to meet the needs of the armed force concerned consistent with the requirement of exemplary conduct."[18]

In late 2019, Congress changed the law to expand the requirement for selection boards to consider adverse information. Prior to this change, adverse information had to be provided to the boards evaluating officers for promotion to the grades of O-7 and above. For officers in lower pay grades, adverse information could be reviewed after the boards had met, and only for those who had been selected. However, Sec. 502 of the fiscal year (FY) 2020 National Defense Authorization Act (NDAA) amended Title 10, Sec. 615, of the U.S. Code to now require active-component promotion boards to consider adverse information for officers being considered for promotion to O-4 and above, and reserve-component promotion boards to consider adverse information for officers being considered for promotion to O-6 and above. Congress amended 10 U.S.C. 615 without amending the parallel reserve provision in 10 U.S.C. 14107.

U.S. Department of Defense Policy

The primary DoD policy implementing statutory provisions in Title 10 of the U.S. Code regarding adverse and reportable information requirements and processes for military officer personnel actions is DoD Instruction (DoDI) 1320.04, *Military Officer Actions Requiring Presidential, Secretary of Defense, or Under Secretary of Defense for Personnel and Readiness Approval or Senate Confirmation*.[19] This policy explains the process and timelines for the approval and confirmation packages, defines adverse and reportable information, specifies which databases must be checked for adverse or reportable information, explains how such information should be managed, and lists what documents are required for the personnel packages. Under DoDI 1320.04, for G/FO personnel actions, the relevant military department secretaries must certify that the officers are "mentally, physically, morally, and professionally qualified for promotion or appointment."[20] They must also certify the following statement to OSD, the President, and the Senate regarding the service files for the nominated officers:

> The files contain no adverse information about this/these officer(s) since his/her/their last Senate confirmation. Further, to the best of my knowledge, there is no planned or ongoing

---

[17] 10 U.S.C. 615; 10 U.S.C. 14107.

[18] 10 U.S.C. 616(c)(3); 10 U.S.C. 14108(b)(3).

[19] DoDI 1320.04, 2014. Current DoD and service policies relating to adverse and reportable information originated following a dispute between DoD leadership and the SASC regarding an Army general officer nomination in 1988 (Harrell and Hix, 2012, pp. 5–8). This led to the promulgation of a new DoD policy in September 1988 by then–Secretary of Defense Frank Carlucci. The new policy required future nominations of one- and two-star officers to include a certification by the military department secretary that service records had been checked for adverse information and that there was no "evidence of misconduct" or "pending investigation[s] of alleged misconduct" with respect to the nominees (Secretary of Defense, "General and Flag Officer Nominations," memorandum for the Secretary of the Army, Washington, D.C., September 2, 1988a). This policy was formalized in a March 1995 revision to DoDI 1320.4, which was then updated in 2014, becoming DoDI 1320.04.

[20] DoDI 1320.04, 2014, p. 2.

investigation or inquiry into matters that constitute alleged adverse information on the part of this/these officer(s).[21]

This overarching policy is discussed in greater detail later in this report.

The 2010 RAND Review on Adverse and Reportable Information Regarding General and Flag Officers

The 2014 version of the overarching policy (DoDI 1320.04) includes language intended to address findings from RAND's 2010 evaluation of previous guidance.[22] That assessment identified and reviewed the various policies and processes within OSD and the Services for managing adverse and reportable information relevant to decisions regarding the promotion, assignment, and retirement of G/FOs. The report contained flow charts summarizing the processes; detailed strengths, shortcomings, and differing perceptions surrounding these policies and processes; and offered recommendations. Highlights are summarized in this section.

Key Findings Regarding Policies and Processes in 2010

RAND's 2010 assessment found that the 1995 version of the overarching policy, which was then DoDI 1320.4 (and has been known as DoDI 1320.04 since it was updated in 2014), needed a formal update to integrate content from several subsequent supplemental memoranda. RAND's assessment also noted that greater specification of certain issues would aid the policy's implementation. For example, it noted the need to better clarify what constitutes reportable information. Additionally, although the DoD policy did refer specifically to information in the EEO files that track complaints by civilian employees, it did not similarly call out equal opportunity (EO) complaints by military personnel as a potential source of investigations, so there was no explicit requirement to check the latter. The review also found some differing information or levels of specification between DoD guidance and Chairman of the Joint Chiefs of Staff Instruction (CJCSI) 1331.01D, *Manpower and Personnel Actions Involving General and Flag Officers*, such as their explanations of reportable information.[23]

At the Service level at that time, there was written guidance on different parts of the processes for managing G/FOs, but no Service had complete detailed guidance on all of the steps for all of the personnel processes (assigning, promoting, and retiring these senior officers). The RAND assessment found that the adverse and reportable information reporting processes for G/FOs differed across the Services and that none of the Service personnel involved with these processes had either expertise in or the designated responsibility for the entire process.

In 2010, the RAND research team also identified ways that processes could be improved to ensure consistency and compliance with DoD or Senate intentions. The team found that the Services were not consistently checking both the EEO and MEO data files for adverse or reportable information. Personnel involved in the process did not always clearly understand the difference between EEO and MEO, and database insufficiencies hampered checks as well.

---

[21] DoDI 1320.04, 2014, p. 19.

[22] Harrell and Hix, 2012.

[23] CJCSI 1331.01D, *Manpower and Personnel Actions Involving General and Flag Officers*, Washington, D.C.: Joint Chiefs of Staff, August 1, 2010, certified current as of February 11, 2013.

Additionally, although DoD IG screens were supposed to be completed before and after G/FO selection boards, they were not being done consistently before selection boards for O-6 officers (who are field-grade officers) being considered for promotion to O-7 (G/FOs).

At that time, the level of detail on adverse or reportable information provided to the selection boards and promotion review boards varied. Selection boards reviewed only brief summaries that some personnel were concerned could be "written to minimize or deemphasize the adverse nature of the individual case."[24] Regarding promotion review boards, some received complete investigations, some redacted reports, and some only one-page summaries.

The RAND report also noted that DoD and SASC processes for reviewing and evaluating unfavorable information appeared to be guided by different philosophies. DoD focused on incidents within the past ten years or since the last personnel action that could be substantiated or disproved and that could be judged under established regulations and standards. Interviews with SASC professional staff, however, suggested that senators were interested in evaluating the individual as a whole—especially an officer's judgment, regardless of whether the actions violated policy—and in understanding the individual's entire record, not just the recent decade or period since that person's last evaluation. Additionally, whereas the DoD system did not call for differential scrutiny by pay grade, SASC perspectives suggested applying greater scrutiny and lower tolerance for mistakes or misconduct when evaluating the more senior G/FOs. Another significant distinction was that the SASC wanted to review commander letters of counseling or other professional development communication intended to address an officer's lapse in judgment, but the Services considered those to be private communications that should not be weighed in promotion decisions regarding G/FOs. Finally, perspectives differed regarding the review of officers' files: SASC staff asserted that Service representatives should read all investigation files, including the investigation report and supporting materials, while Service representatives maintained that most cases required only a review of the investigation report, and some cases even appeared self-evident from just the investigation summary.

Recommendations from the 2010 Review

The 2010 RAND review recommended several changes to policy. It recommended that OSD and the Joint Staff update their guidance to clarify the definition of *reportable information*, the means by which this information is updated and distributed to the relevant offices, and the processes for considering it in selection, promotion, and retirement of G/FOs. In terms of processes, the RAND report suggested that each Service name a party responsible for the entire nomination and retirement process for G/FOs, including how adverse and reportable information is handled. The Services also needed to ensure that they satisfied all requirements for prescreening officers eligible for promotion, including the required IG, MEO, and EEO data file checks. Additionally, the report recommended that the Services provide all promotion selection boards with a consistent and sufficient amount of detail to objectively characterize any adverse information and consistently provide all promotion review boards with the complete investigative materials.

The RAND report also recommended that law and policy continue to allow for the private counseling of G/FOs when appropriate without the risk that the incident or counseling could end up in a nomination package or requested by the SASC. DoD and the SASC were

---

[24] Harrell and Hix, 2012, p. 42.

encouraged to discuss their other differing perspectives regarding adverse information processes. Finally, the report recommended that the Service personnel read the complete investigative materials for each adverse case unless they explicitly determine that a complete reading is not required for a specific case that is self-evident.

Rationale for a Research Update

As introduced in Chapter One, there were several rationales for revisiting these policies and processes in 2019—specifically, that enough time had passed since the policy updates in 2014 to expose any remaining ambiguities or conflicts that could be addressed; that the previous assessment focused on the management of only G/FOs; that military officer conduct remained a Service, DoD, and SASC concern; and that the SASC had recommended the study be updated.

Evaluation of Updates to Policy and Process and Expansion of Scope

After the 2010 RAND review focused on G/FO policies and processes was completed, a DoD and Service working group met to review the findings and recommendations, solicit additional feedback, and discuss the way forward. One outcome of these RAND and working group reviews was OSD's 2014 update of the 1995 DoDI 1320.4. The updated instruction includes much more specific information and is nearly double the length of the 1995 version. The new DoDI elaborates on the definitions of adverse and reportable information.[25] These definitions are discussed in Chapter Three.

The 2014 version of the DoDI also clarifies that the military department secretaries must certify that *all* active and reserve officers who are nominated or recommended for promotion or appointment *to any pay grade* meet the exemplary conduct standards, regardless of any adverse information.[26] The revised policy also specifically names the investigative files that the Services should check before forwarding an officer personnel action for DoD or Presidential approval or Senate confirmation, including MEO and EEO.[27]

DoDI 1320.04 requires that the policy be reissued, cancelled, or certified current within five years of its issue. DoD had identified a few issues it wanted to address through an update, so for DoD's consideration this 2019 assessment gathered additional feedback on the experiences of those who have been referencing and implementing the policy.

Continued Concerns Regarding Military Officer Misconduct and Adverse and Reportable Information Reporting

Several prominent cases in the past have caused concern regarding adverse information and the processes for selection, promotion, confirmation, and assignment of military officers, and cases continue to emerge today. One of the significant historical cases that had a lasting impact is the 1991 public scandal emerging from the Navy and Marine Corps aviators' annual Tailhook convention in Las Vegas. Tailhook generated enormous congressional interest, including a

---

[25] DoDI 1320.04, 2014, pp. 16–17. As of the end of 2019, CJCSI 1331.01D had not yet been updated; Joint Staff representatives informed us that revisions were pending.

[26] DoDI 1320.04, 2014, pp. 11, 17, 35, 49, 53–54.

[27] DoDI 1320.04, 2014, p. 19.

decision by the SASC to place a hold on promotions for 4,500 Navy and Marine Corps officers until the extent of their actions at Tailhook could be determined.[28] Many officers were eventually disciplined, including being denied promotions or command assignments, and information about Tailhook involvement was reported to the Senate for many years after the scandal.[29] More recently, in the wake of the Army's Abu Ghraib scandal and public outcry regarding detainee abuse more broadly,[30] during the confirmation process the Senate has scrutinized officers' involvement in detention or interrogation operations. Scrutiny has also focused on personal ethics and conduct, including recent and ongoing investigations of the involvement of Navy officers in the Glenn-Defense Marine Asia (GDMA) corruption scandal (also known as the "Fat Leonard" scandal after the nickname for GDMA President and Chief Executive Officer Leonard Glenn Francis).[31]

Furthermore, the Senate has taken increasing interest in officers' records with respect to sexual misconduct, including accusations directed at those officers,[32] and officers' roles and responsibilities in cases being adjudicated or in their oversight of the military justice system.[33] Senators have also expressed interest in other types of issues or incidents, such as alleged falsification of nuclear proficiency test results by Air Force units.[34]

In light of these recent high-profile cases of officer misconduct, the research sponsor indicated to us that the SASC had encouraged DoD to update the 2010 review of policies and processes regarding the management of adverse and reportable information regarding military officers.

---

[28]   Rowan Scarborough, "10,000 Navy Jobs Cut: The Reason—Tailhook or Politics?" *Washington Times,* June 30, 1992; see also Dan Balz, "Thomas Hearings Resonate Across U.S.: Harassment Controversy Highlights Political, Cultural, Class Divisions, *Washington Post,* October 17, 1991.

[29]   See Kingsley R. Browne, "Military Sex Scandals from Tailhook to the Present: The Cure Can Be Worse Than the Disease," *Duke Journal of Gender Law & Policy,* Vol. 14, 2007, which cites Rowan Scarborough, "Navy Chief Reverses: Won't Promote Pilot Cleared in Tailhook," *Washington Times,* December 29, 1995; Rowan Scarborough, "Tailhook Officer Gives Up Fight for Promotion, Retires: Navy Officials Relieved That Battle Is Over," *Washington Times,* July 13, 1996a; and Rowan Scarborough, "Lawmakers Ease Tailhook Promotions: Panel Also Orders Process to Help Officers Answer Charges," *Washington Times,* September 28, 1996b.

[30]   For example, see the publicly available redacted version of Office of the Inspector General of the Department of Defense, *Review of DoD-Directed Investigations of Detainee Abuse (U),* Arlington, Va., Report No. 06-INTEL-10, August 25, 2006a. (The notice of declassification is located at Office of the Inspector General of the Department of Defense, "Review of DoD-Directed Investigations of Detainee Abuse (U) (Redacted)," webpage, August 25, 2006b.)

[31]   For highlights, see "Glenn Defense Marine Asia and the US 7th Fleet (the 'Fat Leonard' Scandal)," *Compendium of Arms Trade Corruption,* webpage, last updated November 26, 2018.

[32]   For example, the recent case of Air Force Gen John Hyten, while he was being considered by the Senate for confirmation as vice chairman of the Joint Chiefs of Staff, illustrates the heightened scrutiny attending such allegations. See Karoun Demirjian, "A Colonel Accused a Four-Star General of Sexual Assault. A Senate Panel Will Decide What Happens Next," *Washington Post,* July 28, 2019; see also Karoun Demirjian, "Senate Armed Services Panel Votes to Advance Trump's Pick to Be Military's No. 2, Despite Sexual Assault Allegations," *Washington Post,* July 31, 2019.

[33]   See Rebecca Kheel, "Gillibrand Tears into Army Nominee over Military Sexual Assault: 'You're Failing Us,'" *The Hill,* May 2, 2019 (reporting on Sen. Kirsten Gillibrand's criticism at the confirmation hearing for GEN James McConville to become the next Army chief of staff, regarding the Pentagon's release of data showing a 38-percent jump in instances of military sexual assault over the preceding two years); see also Meghann Myers, "Gillibrand Grills Next Army Chief on Rise of Sexual Assaults, Decrease in Prosecutions," *Army Times,* May 2, 2019.

[34]   See Dan Lamothe, "Exclusive: Nuke Cheating Scandal Puts Promotions for Air Force Brass on Ice," *Foreign Policy,* January 30, 2014.

Summary

The legal bases for appointing or commissioning military officers rest in the Constitution and the U.S. Code. The primary overarching policy that describes how the Services and DoD will comply with the law is DoDI 1320.04, *Military Officer Actions Requiring Presidential, Secretary of Defense, or Under Secretary of Defense for Personnel and Readiness Approval or Senate Confirmation.*

In compliance with the law and DoD policy, promotions and selection boards recommend officers for promotion and take into consideration any adverse information in the officer's background. As of 2019, active-component promotion boards are required to consider adverse information for officers who are candidates for promotion to O-4 and above, and reserve-component promotion boards are to consider adverse information for candidates for promotion to O-6 and above.

A RAND review in 2010 of policies and processes about adverse and reportable information for G/FOs identified ambiguity on what constitutes reportable information; instances where DoD, Chairman of the Joint Chiefs of Staff (CJCS), or Service policies were not fully consistent or aligned; and a lack of visibility into the complete chain of processes for officer personnel packages. It also highlighted a few instances in which database checks for adverse or reportable information could be more complete or consistent, as well as inconsistencies in the detail or type of information provided to promotion selection and review boards. Additionally, the evaluation revealed that DoD and the SASC were guided by different philosophies when reviewing officers' personnel packages. Notably, this report recommended preserving military commanders' ability to counsel their officers privately, without the risk that that information would appear in officers' nomination packages.

DoD requested an update to this RAND assessment for several reasons. It has been nearly a decade since the previous review, and DoD and Service policies and processes regarding adverse and reportable information have been revised since; most notably, the updated overarching DoD policy was published in 2014. Additionally, as a starting point, the previous study focused on policies and processes pertaining to G/FOs, but there was a need for a similar assessment for officer pay grades O-6 and below. Furthermore, documenting and evaluating misconduct among U.S. military officers remains a Service, DoD, and SASC concern, especially in light of certain serious and high-profile cases. Additionally, the SASC recommended that DoD review the current processes to ensure that they align with statutory requirements.

CHAPTER THREE

2014 Updated U.S. Department of Defense Definitions of Adverse and Reportable Information and Reporting Requirements

In 2014, DoD published a revised instruction, DoDI 1320.04, *Military Officer Actions Requiring Presidential, Secretary of Defense, or Under Secretary of Defense for Personnel and Readiness Approval or Senate Confirmation.*[1] Some personnel actions—such as retirement of officers in pay grades O-9 and O-10 when there is no adverse or reportable information and no need for a service-in-grade waiver—can be approved at the OSD level. For appointments of active-component officers to the grades of O-1 through O-3 and reserve-component officers grades O-1 to O-5, the President has delegated the appointment authority to the Secretary of Defense.[2] Other types of actions, such as appointments to any of the G/FO grades, need OSD endorsement, Presidential approval, and Senate confirmation.

The Services must provide proposed military officer personnel action packages for higher-level review. DoD guidance in DoDI 1320.04 on preparing these packages describes not only what information DoD needs for its own review but also what is expected by the President and the Senate. The details of what must be included in these personnel packages vary by the type of action (e.g., promotion packages need to include details about the associated promotion selection boards, special selection boards, or promotion review boards). However, key elements required of personnel packages more generally that are relevant for our study include

- a memorandum from the secretary of the military department, including a discussion of any adverse or reportable information, and an exemplary conduct certification to support any favorable personnel actions
- a CJCS memorandum or coordination on the secretary's memorandum
- documentation from a DoD Office of the Inspector General (OIG) database check not more than 90 days old
- for packages reporting adverse or reportable information:
    - an adverse information summary sheet, a reportable information summary sheet, or both (see Appendix B for DoD's templates)
    - a complete, unredacted report of the investigation, any punitive letters, statements by the officers, and nonjudicial punishment proceedings.

Key updates included in 2014 DoD guidance are expanded definitions of this "adverse" and "reportable" information that must be reported in these packages. The purpose of these

---

[1] As mentioned earlier, the previous version of the instruction (DoDI 1320.4) was published in 1995.

[2] U.S. Government Accountability Office, *Military Personnel: Factors Affecting Approval Time for Officer Appointments,* Washington, D.C., GAO-19-527R, June 27, 2019, p. 13.

revisions was to provide greater clarity to the offices that apply the policy in an effort to improve compliance and consistency in the reporting process. This chapter describes the changes to those definitions. It also documents feedback from personnel in offices responsible for implementing this policy that helps pinpoint where further refinements might be helpful for ensuring the policies are interpreted and applied as intended.

New Definitions

The 2014 updated instruction (DoDI 1320.04) expanded the definitions for two key terms: *adverse information* and *reportable information*. These are two types of unfavorable or potentially unfavorable information that need to be documented and reported so that military and SASC decisionmakers can weigh them when evaluating proposed personnel actions, such as appointments, promotions, and retirements.

Adverse Information

Figure 3.1 displays the DoD definition of adverse information as of 2014 and issues that will be discussed in this section.

Figure 3.1
U.S. Department of Defense Definition of *Adverse Information* and Issues Raised by Offices That Apply It

What about unsubstantiated findings that reflect questions of judgment? →

A substantiated adverse finding or conclusion from an officially documented investigation or inquiry or any other credible information of an adverse nature. To be credible, the information must be resolved and supported by a preponderance of the evidence. To be adverse, the information must be derogatory, unfavorable, or of a nature that reflects clearly unacceptable conduct, integrity or judgment on the part of the individual. The following types of information, even though credible, are not considered adverse:

← *Is the intent to exclude "probable cause," a lower threshold of proof than "preponderance of the evidence"?*

- Motor vehicle violations that did not require a court appearance.
- Minor infractions without negative effect on an individual or the good order and discipline of the organization that:

Do one or both conditions need to be met to exclude it? →

  - Were not identified as a result of substantiated findings or conclusions from an officially documented investigation.
  - Did not result in more than a non-punitive rehabilitative counseling administered by a superior to a subordinate.

- Information previously considered by the Senate pursuant to a prior appointment of the officer.

← *Clarify with the Services that in some cases the SASC will want to (re)review older information, but that these definitions still align with Senate expectations.*

- Information attributed to an individual 10 or more years before the date of the personnel action under consideration, except for substantiated conduct any single act of which, if tried by court-martial, could have resulted in the imposition of a punitive discharge and confinement for more than 1 year. The date of the substantiated adverse finding or conclusion from an officially documented investigation or inquiry is used to establish the time period, not the date of the incident.

SOURCE: DoDI 1320.04, 2014, p. 16; annotations and highlighting added by the authors.

The 1995 DoDI contained a concise definition of adverse information: "Any substantiated adverse finding or conclusion from an officially documented investigation or inquiry."[3] The 2014 policy provides additional detail on what this definition covers and what does not rise to the level of being adverse. The expanded definition appends "or any other credible information of an adverse nature."[4] The policy then proceeds to explain what is meant by *credible* and *adverse.*

The current definition states, "To be credible, the information must be resolved and supported by a preponderance of the evidence."[5] Representatives working in one Service office that applies this policy said that there had been some debate across offices in that Service about whether the intent of the policy was to exclude information with a probable cause determination—a lower threshold of proof than preponderance of the evidence,[6] yet one that can require law enforcement or criminal investigative organizations to register (title and index) the individual in the Defense Central Index of Investigations.[7] Such a charge might never be proven by a higher standard, or the individual might later be found not guilty, but by policy the information describing the individual as the subject of a criminal investigation will remain in the index (unless there was a case of mistaken identity or a lack of credible information at the time of titling and indexing). Without explicitly clarifying whether probable cause investigative information should be considered adverse, the policy leaves open the possibility that different offices will make different assumptions about policymaker expectations when determining what to report.

In defining *adverse,* DoDI 1320.04 includes information that is derogatory, is unfavorable, or reflects "clearly unacceptable conduct" or unacceptable "integrity or judgment." The revised

---

[3]   DoDI 1320.4, *Military Officer Actions Requiring Approval of the Secretary of Defense or the President, or Confirmation by the Senate,* Washington, D.C.: U.S. Department of Defense, March 14, 1995, p. 2.

[4]   DoDI 1320.04, 2014, p. 16.

[5]   DoDI 1320.04, 2014, p. 16.

[6]   The probable cause standard is rooted in the Fourth Amendment to the Constitution, which states that

> [t]he right of the people to be secure in their persons, houses, papers, and effects, against unreasonable searches and seizures, shall not be violated, and no Warrants shall issue, *but upon probable cause,* supported by Oath or affirmation, and particularly describing the place to be searched, and the persons or things to be seized. (U.S. Constitution, Philadelphia, Pa., 1788, Amendment 4, 1791; emphasis added)

The *probable cause* standard has evolved as a reasonable basis threshold for law enforcement activity, such as arrests, searches, or seizures, and is understood to fall somewhere between *no evidence* and a *preponderance of the evidence,* meaning a greater-than-50-percent chance that the claim is true. The Supreme Court has wrestled with its definition of probable cause, stating recently that it "deals with probabilities and depends on the totality of the circumstances" and is "'a fluid concept' that is 'not readily, or even usefully, reduced to a neat set of legal rules" (*District of Columbia v. Wesby,* 138 S. Ct. 577, 586 [2018]). Probable cause "requires only a probability or substantial chance of criminal activity, not an actual showing of such activity" (*Illinois v. Gates,* 462 U.S. 213, 243–244 [1983]). In the military justice system, probable cause exists in the search context "where there is a reasonable belief that the person, property, or evidence sought is located in the place or on the person to be searched" (Military Rules of Evidence 315[f][2]).

[7]   DoDI 5505.07, *Titling and Indexing in Criminal Investigations,* Washington, D.C.: U.S. Department of Defense, February 28, 2018, p. 3. DoD's instruction requires that "subjects of criminal investigations" be titled and indexed "as soon as the investigation determines there is credible information that the subject committed a criminal offense." This standard is further defined as "[i]nformation . . . that, considering the source and nature of the information and the totality of the circumstances, is sufficiently believable to lead a trained criminal investigator to presume the fact or facts in question are true." This "credible information" standard is understood within the military law enforcement and legal communities to be roughly equivalent to the probable cause standard in civilian law enforcement, existing somewhere on a spectrum above no evidence but well below the standard of preponderance of the evidence.

definition more closely aligns DoD policy with the previously documented SASC expectations about the adverse information reporting process by moving beyond a more-narrowly focused incident-based approach (conduct) toward a more holistic understanding of an individual's overall suitability and exemplary conduct (including integrity and judgment).[8] Although the updated definition is clearly more comprehensive than the previous version, one compliance challenge noted by SASC staff is cases in which the allegation was unsubstantiated (i.e., the officer was cleared of that particular charge) but the investigative files reveal credible evidence of the officer exhibiting poor judgment or other inappropriate behaviors. SASC staff emphasized that officer personnel packages that do not treat such cases as adverse information fall short of SASC expectations and do a disservice to the senior leaders making decisions about their officers.

DoDI 1320.04 further outlines the types of information that are *not* considered adverse for reporting purposes (even if credible), such as motor vehicle violations that do not require a court appearance and certain types of minor infractions that do not affect good order and discipline.[9] Personnel in multiple offices that apply DoDI 1320.04 pointed us to the two bulleted conditions listed under "minor infractions without negative effect on an individual or the good order and discipline of the organization" (see Figure 3.1). They reported that there had been confusion about whether the language meant that one of those conditions must be met or that both must be met to exclude an action as adverse. Although DoD has been able to provide clarification to such inquiries, the point remains relevant for the next policy iteration.

DoDI 1320.04's definition of *adverse* also permits the exclusion of incidents that resulted in no more than nonpunitive rehabilitative counseling; this definition introduces opportunities for inconsistent reporting of adverse information across officers and across Services. The policy permits behaviors to be reported as adverse for some officers but not for others on the basis of the type of action their superiors took.

The instruction further excludes information previously considered by the Senate for an earlier nomination of the officer, which is information that also would have been previously considered by the Services and DoD. The definition also limits the time period of consideration to findings or conclusions reached in the previous ten years (although exceptions are also stated). OSD and the Services reported that there have been additional cases, however, in which the Senate has requested information previously reviewed or older than ten years. Offices in the Services asked whether this meant that the policy was outdated and the SASC expects to receive all past information that had been considered adverse. SASC representatives confirmed, however, that these two exclusions generally comport with SASC expectations, but there will occasionally be cases in which the SASC will want to review or rereview older information.

Reportable Information

In addition to adverse information, DoDI 1320.04 outlines other types of unfavorable information that need to be reported in officer personnel packages for consideration. The 1995 DoDI did not include a reportable information category as the 2014 DoDI does, but it referred to "alleged adverse information," which it defined as follows:

---

[8]   Harrell and Hix, 2012, p. xiii.

[9]   DoDI 1320.04, 2014, p. 16.

Any allegation of conflict of interest, failure to adhere to required standards of conduct, abuse of authority, misconduct or information serving as the basis for an incomplete or unresolved official investigation or inquiry into a possible conflict of interest or failure to adhere to standards of conduct or misconduct.[10]

The previous version of the policy also explained that

[n]ormally, the Department of Defense does not report alleged adverse information or other unsubstantiated allegations to the Senate. However, in extraordinary cases, such as where the allegations received significant media attention or when the Senate Armed Service Committee (SASC) brings allegations to the attention of the Department of Defense, the Secretaries of the Military Departments shall include a discussion of the unsubstantiated allegations in the nomination package.[11]

The 2010 RAND assessment documented questions about the policy that had emerged. For example, for ongoing investigations regarding potential detainee abuse within a unit, there were questions about whether that information was reportable for everyone in the unit and the chain of command above it, regardless of an individual's proximity to the alleged activity. The report recommended that DoD guidance provide greater clarity in its definition of *reportable information* and the means by which updated lists of reportable information (e.g., new topics of interest to the SASC) will be distributed to the offices expected to report the information.

Figure 3.2 displays the updated 2014 policy's elaboration of what constitutes reportable information, as well as opportunities for improvement raised in our meetings with representatives who apply this policy in their specific offices.

As shown in the figure, the 2014 DoDI defines *reportable information* along three dimensions.

First, reportable information includes any information the Senate requests to be reported. If information is requested by members of the Senate, it is the obligation of the Services and DoD to provide it regardless of the nature of that information. There is no central, authoritative list of topics of interest to the Senate posted for or distributed to the relevant offices. There was considerable overlap, however, of examples offered in our meetings by representatives from the Services, DoD, and the SASC and listed in slides that the Officer and Enlisted Personnel Management Office (OEPM) of the Office of the Under Secretary of Defense for Personnel and Readiness (OUSD[P&R]) uses to orient new Service officer management staff to the O-6 and below personnel processes. Examples included information related to involvement with detainee abuse, friendly fire incidents, recruiting improprieties, GDMA corruption, improper handling of nuclear weapons or parts, and incidents resulting from the mismanagement of sexual assault cases (such as improper handling, failure to take action, and setting aside punishments).

Second, reportable information includes any information regarding alleged misconduct currently undergoing an investigation or an administrative or judicial process. We noted a discrepancy in characterizing when an investigation or an administrative or judicial process begins. SASC representatives explained that negative information is considered reportable from

---

[10]   DoDI 1320.4, 1995, p. 2.

[11]   DoDI 1320.4, 1995, p. 6.

Figure 3.2
U.S. Department of Defense Definition of *Reportable Information* and Issues Raised by Offices That Apply It

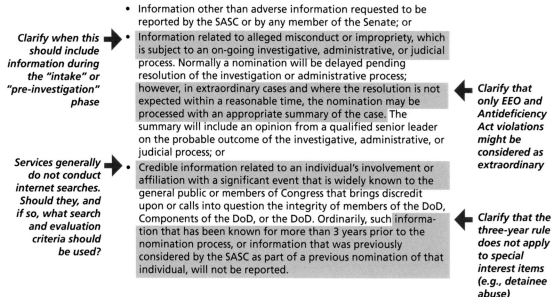

SOURCE: DoDI 1320.04, 2014, p. 16; annotations and highlighting added by the authors.

the point that information is received, especially if the officer's nomination package is already at the White House or the Senate for review. Some Service organizations, however, consider an investigation to be preceded by an "intake" or "pre-investigation" phase, in which a given office establishes whether a given complaint has merit for further investigation and that the intended subject has been accurately identified.[12] Consequently, waiting until a formal investigation is opened can create a delay in notification or result in no notification if the allegation is not investigated further. Senate confidence in these processes can be eroded when the Services are aware of an open allegation against an officer but report it or open a formal investigation only after the Senate votes.

Normally, DoD will not accept nominations for officers who are the subject of an open investigation. The definition notes that, in extraordinary circumstances, the nomination may proceed, and the policy subsequently clarifies what might constitute an extraordinary case: "(e.g., Equal Employment Opportunity complaint or potential Anti-Deficiency Act violation) . . . likely to take months or years to resolve."[13]

Third, reportable information includes credible information of the officer's association with a widely known significant event; in most cases, information older than three years or considered by the SASC for a previous nomination is not considered reportable.[14] However, if the SASC requests older or previously considered information, the information is still consid-

---

[12]   For example, the office might receive a complaint about an officer's alleged impropriety on a U.S. installation, but records reveal that the individual accused of impropriety was overseas at the time of the alleged incident; or, the office might find that the allegation was intended to be against a different individual with a similar name.

[13]   DoDI 1320.04, 2014, p. 17.

[14]   DoDI 1320.04, 2014, pp. 16–17.

ered reportable under the first dimension of reportable information. As noted earlier, there is no official running list of widely known significant events that the SASC considers reportable; however, the Service and DoD offices involved described to us several prominent incidents for which the SASC is interested in officers' involvement or affiliation, even if they were not personally accused of any wrongdoing. The last portion of the definition of reportable information is an addition that more closely aligns the DoD definition with the SASC's intention (i.e., information that could damage the department's reputation, that calls into question personal judgment, or that does both). Note that this definition requires reporting of information that has been known for more than *three years* prior to the nomination process, while the reporting window for adverse information is within *ten years*, but in both cases information previously considered by the SASC does not need to be reported (unless specifically requested).

Summary

The 2014 update to the DoDI provided more-detailed definitions of adverse and reportable information that clarify DoD and SASC expectations. Information from substantiated allegations, topics of interest to the Senate, widely known significant events that reflect poorly on the military, and open investigations on officers is required to supplement officer personnel action packages to provide a more holistic picture of officers' overall behavior and performance when they are under review for appointment, promotion, assignment, or retirement.

CHAPTER FOUR

Personnel Processes

The DoD policy outlining the personnel action processes (DoDI 1320.04, 2014) built upon and expanded the previous policy (DoDI 1320.4, 1995) in multiple ways. The new policy consolidates information from the previous DoDI regarding G/FOs with supplemental guidance that had been published in subsequent memoranda.

The updated DoDI more clearly articulates the responsibilities and authorities for the USD(P&R) and the CJCS. The 1995 DoDI assigned responsibility for ensuring compliance to the Assistant Secretary of Defense for Force Management Policy (an office that was subordinate to the USD[P&R]).[1] The 2014 DoDI assigns compliance responsibilities to the USD(P&R), the secretaries of the military departments, and the CJCS.

The revised policy also more clearly documents the responsibilities for officer personnel packages at the Service, Department, and Joint Chiefs of Staff levels. The updated policy explicitly lists the records that the Services must check for adverse and reportable information for personnel actions for officers in pay grades O-7 and above, requires that the military department secretaries certify that those checks have been completed, and specifies when those checks must be updated. Also, the updated DoDI contains a new enclosure on the reporting requirements for personnel actions for officers in the grades of O-6 and below (Enclosure 6).

This chapter provides a brief overview of the management of adverse and reportable information in each of the processes within the scope of our study as of 2019: officer appointments, promotions, special assignments, and retirements.

As of 2019, policies and personnel processes for officers in pay grades O-6 and below differed in important ways from those for G/FOs (pay grades O-7 to O-10). Additionally, the management of adverse and reportable information for officers in pay grades O-6 and below was not the focus of the 2010 RAND evaluation (with the exception of O-6 officers being considered for promotion to O-7). Therefore, this chapter discusses processes for officers O-6 and below, followed by processes for G/FOs.

Size of the Officer Corps

To provide a sense of the size of the officer corps, Tables 4.1 and 4.2 present the total number of officers in each pay grade by Service and component in 2018. The size of the officer corps

---

[1] DoDI 1320.4, 1995, p. 2. The position of Assistant Secretary of Defense for Force Management Policy was replaced in 2003 by the position of Principal Deputy Under Secretary of Defense for Personnel and Readiness (PDUSD[P&R]) (DoD Directive [DoDD] 5124.8, *Principal Deputy Under Secretary of Defense for Personnel and Readiness (PDUSD(P&R))*, Washington, D.C.: U.S. Department of Defense, July 16, 2003).

Table 4.1
Number of Active-Component Officers by Service and Pay Grade, 2018

Pay Grade	Army	Navy	Marine Corps	Air Force	Total DoD
O-1	9,881	7,018	3,203	7,900	28,002
O-2	11,292	6,659	3,337	6,995	28,283
O-3	28,524	18,726	6,122	20,851	74,223
O-4	15,139	10,592	3,883	13,593	43,207
O-5	8,846	6,668	1,901	9,764	27,179
O-6	4,040	3,125	643	3,241	11,049
O-7	143	107	41	149	440
O-8	122	61	27	90	300
O-9	44	38	21	44	147
O-10	15	8	4	13	40
Total	78,046	53,002	19,182	62,640	212,870

SOURCE: Office of the Deputy Assistant Secretary of Defense for Military Community and Family Policy, *2018 Demographics: Profile of the Military Community*, Washington, D.C.: U.S. Department of Defense, 2019, p. 15.

Table 4.2
Number of Reserve-Component Officers by Component and Pay Grade, 2018

Pay Grade	Army National Guard	Army Reserve	Navy Reserve	Marine Corps Reserve	Air National Guard	Air Force Reserve	Total DoD
O-1	6,744	2,223	415	268	1,099	370	11,119
O-2	7,597	5,570	579	307	1,178	544	15,775
O-3	10,657	10,766	3,487	1,083	3,576	2,847	32,416
O-4	6,724	8,986	4,943	1,564	4,346	4,996	31,559
O-5	3,545	4,833	3,303	689	3,979	3,873	20,222
O-6	1,335	1,850	1,235	289	1,041	1,010	6,760
O-7	165	86	38	6	135	51	481
O-8	80	34	19	5	44	25	207
O-9	3	0	0	1	2	0	6
O-10	0	0	0	0	1	0	1
Total	36,850	34,348	14,019	4,212	15,401	13,716	118,546

SOURCE: Office of the Deputy Assistant Secretary of Defense for Military Community and Family Policy, 2019, p. 67.

in any year may vary because of several factors, including increases or decreases in authorized end strength and recruiting and retention patterns. Although specific data regarding the number of officers considered for promotion each year were not available, these tables show that the number of officers is considerably larger in the lower pay grades than in the G/FO corps. For example, in 2018 there were 927 active-component and 695 reserve-component G/FOs in all of the pay grades O-7 to O-10, but there were 11,049 active-component and 6,760 reserve-component O-6s. Thus, there were more than ten times as many officers in the pay grade preceding the G/FO pay grades than there were G/FOs. Consequently, the scale of the work managing adverse and reportable information for officers O-6 and below is considerably greater than that for G/FOs.

Processes for Officers in Pay Grades O-6 and Below

DoDI 1320.04 (2014) expanded the reporting requirements from the Services to OSD and the Senate beyond the G/FO ranks to officers in the pay grades of O-6 and below (abbreviated as *O6B* in the policy). [2] Original appointments of officers to the grades of O-1 through O-3, promotion appointments to the grades of O-2 and O-3, and reserve O-4 and O-5 appointments require only Presidential approval (delegated to the Secretary of Defense), while personnel actions for active-component officers in the grades of O-4 to O-6 and reserve-component officers in the grade of O-6 require Secretary of Defense endorsement, Presidential approval, and Senate confirmation.[3] The updated policy provides guidelines for circumstances in which the Services should report adverse information for officers in the grades of O-6 and below in Enclosure 6. The policy does not list records that need to be systematically checked for adverse and reportable information for officers in pay grades O-6 and below,[4] because such information for these officers is not universally required.

Although DoD does not typically report adverse information or reportable information to the Senate for nominations to the pay grades of O-6 and below, military department secretaries are instructed to submit adverse information in "extraordinary cases."[5] Extraordinary cases include those in which there is significant media attention or the SASC brings adverse information to DoD's attention. Additionally, the military department secretaries have the discretion to include adverse or reportable information even in cases in which it is not required.

Promotions
In the event that adverse information that is to be reported to OSD is discovered that was not considered in the officer's promotion selection board, special selection board, or federal recognition board, the information will be provided to a promotion review board. In some cases, an officer might have been removed from a previous promotion list; in these instances, the adverse

---

[2] DoDI 1320.04, 2014, Enclosure 6, "Requirements for O6B Actions," p. 34.

[3] See U.S. Code, Title 10, Chapters 33, 36, 69, 1205, and 1403. DoD is not required to use boards for the appointment of officers to the grade of O-1. Under 10 U.S.C. 611 and 14101, DoD is also not required to use boards for promotion to O-2 or O-3; nor do promotions to those grades require Senate confirmation.

[4] The exception would be officers in the pay grade of O-6 who are being considered for promotion to O-7, the first G/FO pay grade.

[5] DoDI 1320.04, 2014, Enclosure 6, "Requirements for O6B Actions," p. 34.

information will be furnished to the next promotion selection board, special selection board, or federal recognition board. The individual officer has the opportunity to provide written comments in response to the adverse or reportable information; the written response will also be supplied to the board. The appropriate board will review the information. If the officer is selected for promotion after a board evaluates the adverse or reportable information, the military department secretary is required to submit a memorandum to OSD along with the officer's materials. In the memorandum, the military department secretary is required to provide both a detailed description about the adverse or reportable information and a specific rationale for why the military department secretary supports the officer. The memorandum of support must address how the officer meets the "requirement of exemplary conduct," as outlined in Title 10 of the U.S. Code.[6] Officer packages for pay grades O-6 and below without adverse or reportable information are then delivered by the military department to OEPM for action by the Deputy Secretary of Defense or the Secretary of Defense; packages provided to OSD with adverse information must instead be addressed to the Secretary of Defense.

Section 502 of the FY 2020 NDAA expands the requirement for furnishing adverse information to promotion selection boards. Previously, adverse information had to be provided to all boards evaluating officers for promotion to O-7 and above. Now, the law requires that adverse information be furnished to all boards selecting active-component officers for promotion to O-4 and above and reserve-component officers for promotion to O-6 and above.[7] Furthermore, the provision requires that adverse information be furnished at every phase of consideration thereafter. Although the provision became effective on the day the FY 2020 NDAA was enacted (December 20, 2019), the Services expressed concerns about the feasibility of performing checks for adverse and reportable information with existing database limitations and funding and manpower allocations, and the Services noted that they will require more resources to meet the new requirements successfully in a timely manner.[8] Previously, for officers being considered for promotion to O-6 and below, the Services checked for adverse and reportable information only after the promotion selection boards had met, and only for the subset of officers selected for promotion. Thus, the new requirement is far more demanding.

Officer Transitions Between Services or Service Components
Transitions between the active component, the reserves, and the National Guard have unique characteristics, considerations, and limitations on data available to the component regarding adverse and reportable information. Officers can transfer between the active component, the Guard, and the Reserve. Within the Guard, officers can transfer between units in different

---

[6]   Title 10 provides three Service-specific references to the requirement for exemplary conduct: 10 U.S.C. 7233 (Army), 10 U.S.C. 8167 (Navy and Marine Corps), and 10 U.S.C. 9233 (Air Force). The statute defines exemplary conduct in four parts, requiring all "commanding officers and others in authority" in a Service

   (1) to show in themselves a good example of virtue, honor, patriotism, and subordination;
   (2) to be vigilant in inspecting the conduct of all persons who are placed under their command;
   (3) to guard against and suppress all dissolute and immoral practices, and to correct, according to the laws and regulations of the . . . [Service], all persons who are guilty of them; and
   (4) to take all necessary and proper measures, under the laws, regulations, and customs of the . . . [Service], to promote and safeguard the morale, the physical well-being, and the general welfare of the officers and enlisted persons under their command or charge.

[7]   Pub. L. 116-92, National Defense Authorization Act for Fiscal Year 2020, December 20, 2019.

[8]   The challenges presented by the new requirement are addressed in more detail in Chapter Six.

states. Although such transitions are most likely to occur at the pay grades of O-6 and below, policy does not prohibit an officer in grades O-7 through O-10 from transferring between components or between interstate Guard assignments.

The names of all officers appointed or promoted in any component must be included on a list of names called a *scroll*.[9] The scroll, along with supporting documentation, is submitted to OSD and distributed to the appropriate office (the Secretary of Defense for officers in the pay grades of O-1 through O-3 in the active component and officers in the pay grades of O-1 through O-5 in the reserve component) or to the White House and the Senate (for officers in the pay grades of O-4 and above in the active component and officers in the pay grades of O-6 and above in the reserve component) for signature. Officers transitioning from the active component to the reserve component must be removed from the active-component list and added to the reserve-component scroll as an original reserve-component appointment.

The procedures for interservice and inter-component transfers are described in a separate policy, DoDI 1300.04.[10] The policy does not discuss adverse or reportable information or exemplary conduct and does not reference DoDI 1320.04. The policy requires mere concurrence by both the gaining Service and the losing Service. The DoD guidance on the original appointment of officers, DoDI 1310.02, requires the military department secretary to provide a "recommendation for an original appointment" memo for original appointments to the Reserve Active Status List; the recommendation must include a forwarding memorandum from the military department secretary with "comments concerning adverse or reportable information in accordance with" DoDI 1320.04, if applicable.[11]

Processes for Federal Recognition Boards for National Guard Officers

The National Guard promotion process begins at the state level, because the guard units belong to the states, but these promotions must be federally recognized in order for the officer to wear the insignia and receive the pay associated with the higher grade when in federal status.[12] 32 U.S.C. 307 defines the requirements by which federal recognition is governed. Upon being federally recognized, officers in the grades of O-1 to O-5 are appointed by the Secretary of Defense, while officers in the grades of O-6 and above are appointed by the President with the advice and consent of the Senate. The National Guard Bureau coordinates the federal recognition process.

Unlike the process for active and reserve officers, officers in the National Guard are promoted to vacancies within a unit, meaning that their promotion is tied to filling a specific position. The officer must have the qualifications prescribed by the military department secretary for the pay grade associated with that position. To determine whether the officer is medically, morally, and professionally qualified for the position, a federal recognition board of

---

[9] DoDI 1320.04, 2014, pp. 60–61.

[10] DoDI 1300.04, *Inter-Service and Inter-Component Transfers of Service Members*, Washington, D.C.: U.S. Department of Defense, July 25, 2017.

[11] DoDI 1310.02, *Original Appointment of Officers*, Washington, D.C.: U.S. Department of Defense, March 26, 2015, p. 13.

[12] The process described here is not required for officers in the active component or the reserves, which are federal organizations.

three officers designated by the military department secretary reviews the individual's file.[13] To recommend officers for federal recognition, the board must certify that the officers meet the exemplary conduct provisions of Title 10, despite any adverse information that may have been reported.[14]

The Chief of the National Guard Bureau is responsible for reviewing the officers' files, board proceedings, and nomination recommendations to determine whether the officers meet the qualifications and requirements for federal recognition or, for the general officer pay grades, for a certificate of eligibility of prequalification (which expedites the process of filling positions at these senior levels).[15] The next steps in the process mirror the active-component promotion approval process. If the officer is being promoted to the pay grade of O-5 or below, the Secretary of Defense approves the federal recognition of the promotion. If the officer is being promoted to the pay grade of O-6 or above, the Deputy Secretary of Defense endorses the package and recommends that the President nominate the officer, with the advice and consent of the Senate, to confirm the officer's federal recognition.[16] For National Guard officers receiving certificates of eligibility for general officer positions, those certificates are valid for two years following Senate confirmation, and the promotion is received only upon filling a position requiring that rank.

For the O-9 and O-10 pay grades, however, there is no federal recognition board or process. A call for nominations is distributed by the state adjutant general. The officer must be nominated by the governor and have the concurrence of the military department secretary. The nomination process proceeds onward in the same way that it does for active-component O-9 and O-10 officers.

DoDI 1320.04 defines the roles for the Services and OSD with respect to the federal recognition process. The military department secretaries are responsible for providing a memorandum that includes a certification that the "officers submitted for promotion meet the exemplary conduct provisions" of Title 10.[17] The USD(P&R) is responsible for reviewing reports of federal recognition boards.[18] The DoDI further requires the Services to include "comments concerning adverse or reportable information" in accordance with the applicable guidance for handling adverse and reportable information for officers promoted to specific grades.[19] For federal recognition of officers to the pay grades of O-1 through O-6, the Services do not conduct the specific adverse and reportable information searches required for promotions to the pay grades of O-7 through O-10.

---

[13] 32 U.S.C. 307.

[14] DoDI 1320.04, 2014, p. 11; 10 U.S.C. 7233; 10 U.S.C. 8167; 10 U.S.C. 9233.

[15] Air National Guard Instruction 36-2501, *General Officer Federal Recognition Boards for General Officer Appointment or Promotion in the Air National Guard*, Arlington, Va.: National Guard Bureau, January 24, 2013; and National Guard Regulation 600-100, *Commissioned Officers Federal Recognition and Related Personnel Actions*, Arlington, Va.: National Guard Bureau, July 6, 2020.

[16] U.S. Government Accountability Office, 2019, p. 2.

[17] DoDI 1320.04, 2014, p. 11; 10 U.S.C. 7233; 10 U.S.C. 8167; 10 U.S.C. 9233.

[18] DoDI 1320.04, 2014, p. 11.

[19] DoDI 1320.04, 2014, p. 53.

Processes for General and Flag Officers

Process Preceding the Selection Board for Promotion to O-7 and O-8

Figure 4.1 captures the existing personnel process preceding the selection boards for the grades of O-7 and O-8.

Consistent with processes at the time of the 2010 RAND review, the process for promotion to O-7 and O-8 begins for all Services with a determination of the promotion zone and thus a determination of the officers eligible for promotion. Previously, following a July 2006 memorandum signed by the USD(P&R),[20] Section 506 of the FY 2006 NDAA amended Title 10 to require that, for G/FOs, "any credible information of an adverse nature, including any substantiated adverse finding or conclusion from an officially documented investigation or inquiry, shall be furnished to the selection board in accordance with the standards and procedures set out in the regulations prescribed by the Secretary of Defense . . . ."[21] DoDI 1320.04 established the standards and procedures for the requirement.[22] DoDI 1320.04 articulates the agency checks and certifications required for O-7 through O-10, including "DoD, Service,

Figure 4.1
Service Personnel Process Preceding the Selection Boards for O-7 and O-8

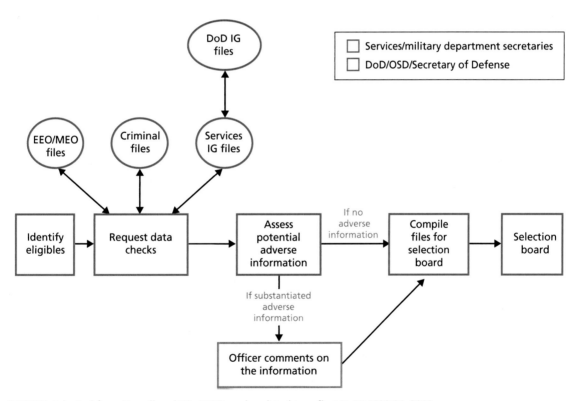

SOURCE: Adapted from Harrell and Hix, 2012, and updated to reflect DoDI 1320.04, 2014.

---

[20] USD(P&R), "General and Flag Officer Boards—Adverse Information of a Credible Nature," memorandum for Secretary of the Army, Secretary of the Navy, Secretary of the Air Force, Chairman of the Joint Chiefs of Staff, Washington, D.C., July 19, 2006.

[21] Public Law 109-163, National Defense Authorization Act for Fiscal Year 2006, January 6, 2006.

[22] DoDI 1320.04, 2014, pp. 19–22.

and State Inspector General files," EEO and MEO databases, the NCIC, the Central Clearance Facility, judge advocate general (JAG) offices, and "other Service database files."[23] The Service is responsible for managing the process; identifying the eligible population for consideration for promotion; and requesting data checks from EEO/MEO, criminal files, Service IG files, and DoD OIG files. The Service then assesses all files for potential adverse or reportable information. If such information is substantiated and meets the DoD definition of adverse, the individual officer is permitted to provide a written comment for the selection board. When adverse information is communicated to the selection board, it is generally provided as a summary.

Each Service conducts preboard screenings of officers identified as candidates for promotion; these screenings are represented in the second box of Figure 4.1, which is connected to the ovals indicating the types of data that must be checked: EEO/MEO files, criminal data files, and Service IG files.[24] Consistent with the processes at the time of the 2010 RAND review, each Service reviews its respective IG files and criminal investigation files and requests DoD OIG file checks.

Following the O-7 and O-8 Selection Board

The Services are responsible for ensuring that the information provided to the General and Flag Officer Matters Office (G/FO Matters) is current and must provide updated DoD OIG notification memoranda to G/FO Matters when information is more than 90 days old.[25] If the DoD OIG finds updated results once a nomination package is received by G/FO Matters, the DoD OIG will provide updated results to G/FO Matters and to the military department until the officer's nomination is confirmed.

If adverse information for a newly selected officer is discovered after the promotion selection board, that information must be considered by a promotion review board, which recommends to the military department secretary whether to support that individual's promotion.[26] The screening process begins immediately following the selection board. The promotion selection board and the military department secretary must certify exemplary conduct of all selected officers. In the case of individuals with adverse or reportable information that has not been previously considered by the Senate, DoD must acknowledge and describe the information to the President and the Senate.[27]

New adverse or reportable information identified during the post-selection board screening may include a new allegation, a new open investigation, and potential adverse or reportable information from a closed investigation. If there is an ongoing investigation, the Service will hold the nomination until the investigation is complete. If the investigation yields substantiated adverse information, the Service will determine whether to support the promotion through a promotion review board. If potential adverse information is identified, the Service provides the

---

[23] DoDI 1320.04, 2014, Enclosure 5, p. 19.

[24] The specific data sources required are described in more detail in Chapter Five.

[25] DoDI 1320.04, 2014, Enclosure 5, p. 19.

[26] Section 505 of the FY 2021 NDAA amended the law to require a special selection review board, rather than a promotion review board, to determine whether the recommendation for promotion should be sustained (Pub. L. 116-283, William M. [Mac] Thornberry National Defense Authorization Act for Fiscal Year 2021, January 1, 2021).

[27] Harrell and Hix, 2012, pp. x, 16–17.

individual with the opportunity to comment on the new information; the information is then provided to a promotion review board to determine whether the Service will support the promotion. If the Service determines that it will support the nomination, the Service submits the nomination package through the standard process, providing the nomination package first to the CJCS to assess for joint requirements and then to OSD to process the promotion package and confirm the documentation. This process is documented in Figure 4.2.

Differences Between O-7 and O-8 Promotions

Consistent with findings in the 2010 RAND review, the promotion process from O-6 to O-7 is typically more burdensome than the promotion process from O-7 to O-8. First, the number of individuals considered for promotion to O-7 is significantly larger than the population considered for promotion to O-8. Second, G/FO management offices across the Services typically maintain a greater degree of awareness of any potentially adverse or reportable information for incidents involving officers in the pay grade of O-7 than for incidents involving officers at the pay grades of O-6 and below. G/FOs work at the highest levels of the military hierarchy, and any allegations of G/FO misconduct must be immediately reported to the DoD OIG for investigation. Third, the most information regarding officers' records will be considered for their appointment to the grade of O-7 because their personnel packages should include any adverse information from the past ten years and any reportable information from the past three years. Because the policy stipulates that information previously considered by the Senate for a prior nomination does not need to be reported, after the promotion to O-7 the personnel packages will typically include only information since that last nomination (unless the Senate requests further information by exception).

Managing Adverse Information Arising After the Services Have Submitted a Package (O-7 to O-10)

If adverse or reportable information is discovered after the military department submits the nomination package to G/FO Matters, the military department may informally request that the nomination package be placed on hold. The same process is followed for all officer nominations in the grades of O-7 through O-10. If the Service identifies any adverse or reportable information (to include pending alleged adverse information or an investigation not previously reported on an officer being nominated), the military department must informally notify G/FO Matters within five duty days of the receipt of the adverse or reportable information.[28] The Service provides the officer's name and grade, the first name on the associated list or scroll,[29] a synopsis of the information or investigation, and the current status of the information. DoDI 1320.04 states that an email from either the director or the deputy director of a military department's G/FO management office is an "acceptable means of making this initial notification."[30] In cases in which more than one officer's name is listed on a scroll, the military department is required to state whether it would prefer that G/FO Matters proceeds with

---

[28] DoDI 1320.04, 2014, Enclosure 5, p. 20.

[29] The current decision support system does not have an individual officer file search capability. All officer scrolls are searchable only by the first name listed on a given scroll. Therefore, to search for the scroll in which an officer is listed, the Service must provide OEPM with both the name of the officer in question and the first name listed on the associated scroll.

[30] DoDI 1320.04, 2014, Enclosure 5, p. 20.

Figure 4.2
Service and U.S. Department of Defense Personnel Process Following the Selection Boards for O-7 and O-8

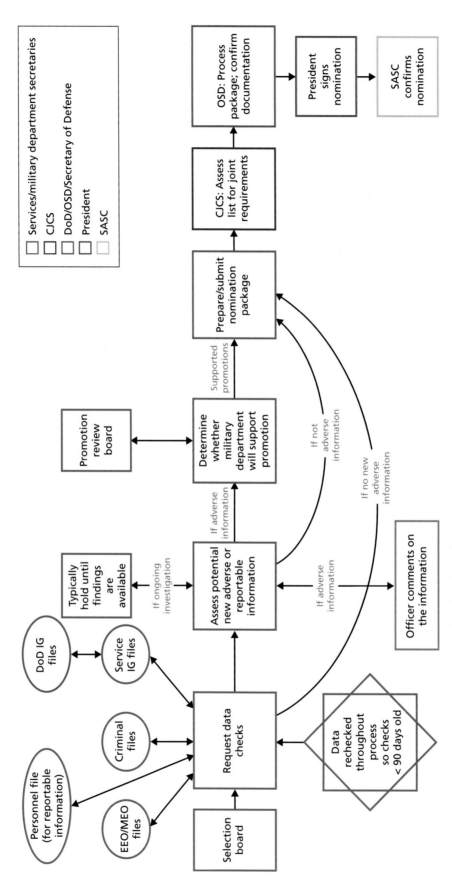

SOURCE: Adapted from Harrell and Hix, 2012, and updated to reflect DoDI 1320.04, 2014.

the remaining names on the list without the name of the officer involved or whether it would prefer for the entire list to be placed on hold.

Once G/FO Matters places an officer's nomination on hold, and in concurrence with the Secretary of Defense and the White House, G/FO Matters will advise the SASC of the information and request that the officer's nomination be placed on hold until the matter is resolved. Using the recommendation of the military department secretary, G/FO Matters will also specify to the SASC whether the remaining officers on the scroll should continue forward for confirmation. If a nomination has already reached the White House or the Senate when adverse or reportable information is discovered, the military department must notify G/FO Matters. If the DoD OIG discovers adverse or reportable information once a nomination has moved forward, it will notify G/FO Matters.

The DoDI further stipulates that the military department secretary must forward a formal notification to G/FO Matters within five days of the initial notification.[31]

Once an investigation has been completed for the officer whose nomination is on hold, the military department secretary will inform the Secretary of Defense in writing through the CJCS and the USD(P&R). The military department secretary must state whether the allegations were substantiated or unsubstantiated, and, in cases in which the allegations are substantiated, the notification must include what action was taken.[32] The military department secretary must further state whether they still support the officer's nomination and must provide an assessment of the officer's judgment (in a similar fashion outlined in the O-6 and below promotions section earlier in the chapter).

G/FO Matters then processes a nomination once the military department has certified the investigation outcome from the DoD OIG. In some cases, the DoD OIG review does not match the military department's findings; in those cases, G/FO Matters continues to hold the nomination until the disparity is resolved. If the disparity cannot be resolved, the military department secretary provides notification and an explanation of the difference to OUSD(P&R). G/FO Matters will then include the military department's explanation in the nomination package.

In some cases, reportable information is discovered that was previously unknown to the officer who is or was under investigation. In those cases, the military department secretary is responsible for ensuring that the officer is made aware of the reportable information and provides the officer with the opportunity to submit a written response to the information. The information and the officer's response will be provided to a promotion review board.

Certain types of reportable information, such as EEO complaints, can create a situation in which the investigative process is likely to take months or years to resolve.[33] In these cases, the military department secretary may submit a nomination package if a preliminary review of the investigation indicates that the case will most likely not be substantiated.[34] The military department secretary will examine the details of the case, any current information provided

[31] DoDI 1320.04, 2014.

[32] DoDI 1320.04, 2014, Enclosure 5, p. 21.

[33] The challenges associated with EEO complaints are addressed more in depth in Chapter Five.

[34] An example would be if an officer was listed in an EEO complaint in which an entire chain of command was listed, but the officer did not have any personal involvement in the reported incident.

through ongoing investigations, the expected length to resolve, and the impact of the nomination not being forwarded.

Role of the Chairman of the Joint Chiefs of Staff in Processing Nominations (O-7 to O-10)

As was the case at the time of the previous RAND review in 2010, once the Services have compiled the materials selected for each of the selectees, the nomination packages are forwarded to the Joint Staff. The role of the CJCS is articulated in CJCSI 1330.01D, *Manpower and Personnel Actions Involving General and Flag Officers*, published in 2010. Additionally, DoDI 1320.04 more clearly articulates the CJCS role than did its 1995 predecessor, DoDI 1320.4.

The CJCS reviews reports of promotion selection boards and special selection boards that considered joint officers, and it reviews and provides advice on O-7 through O-10 nominations and retirement requests.[35] DoDI 1320.04 stipulates that the CJCS will review and comment on all G/FO promotions, nominations, and retirement packages containing adverse or reportable information.[36] The Joint Staff G/FO Matters office is the main point of contact between the Services and the Joint Staff.

CJCS 1331.01D describes the minimum information required in a nomination package. Although the CJCS's review is intended to ensure joint requirement completion, the CJCS also reviews any adverse information and ensures that IG checks are less than 90 days old. Because this policy has not been updated since the 2010 RAND review, the following information required by this policy remains unchanged:

1. a memorandum from the military department secretary addressing any significant aspects of the list of selectees, including any promotion objectives that were not met, actions taken to prevent subsequent failures, or waiver requests
2. the entire selection board report
3. a list of officers considered who currently or previously served on the Joint Staff
4. selection board joint statistics
5. selection list with resumes of officers selected
6. CJCS's letter designating the joint representative
7. joint duty assignment waivers requested
8. adverse information summaries and reports of investigations for officers with adverse information
9. documents required by the Secretary of Defense:
   a. a copy of the scroll for the President's signature
   b. press release
   c. current IG check, not more than 90 days old[37]
   d. draft memorandum to the President
   e. acquisition corps statistics and documentation of coordination with the Under Secretary of Defense (Acquisition, Technology, and Logistics)
   f. ethnic and racial profile statistics

---

[35] DoDI 1320.04, 2014, Enclosure 2, p. 9.

[36] DoDI 1320.04, 2014, Enclosure 2, p. 10.

[37] DoDI 1320.04 specifies that the IG check required is the DoD OIG check.

     g. promotion board report for Secretary of Defense approval

     h. promotion board proceedings.[38]

Once the CJCS coordination is complete, the packages proceed to G/FO Matters for processing.

Appointments and Promotions to O-9 and O-10

Appointments to positions in the grades of O-9 and O-10 differ significantly from promotions to the grades of O-7 and O-8. While officers are promoted to the grades of O-7 and O-8 through formal promotion boards, nominations to the grades of O-9 and O-10 are *positional*; that is, the grade is tied to the specific statutorily designated position for which an officer is nominated. An officer is not promoted to O-9 or O-10 unless appointed to a position requiring an officer in that pay grade. Officers also may be nominated to a new position within their current grade of O-9 or O-10. Figure 4.3 depicts the process through which the Services manage nominations for the grades of O-9 and O-10.

As depicted in Figure 4.3, the process begins when the Service or the Joint Staff identifies a current or projected vacancy. In the case of a joint vacancy, the process is initiated by a request for nomination from the Joint Staff. For vacancies within a Service, the Service Chief (supported by the Service G/FO management office) selects candidates for a specific vacancy. Once a candidate is identified to fill a vacancy, the Service manages the adverse and reportable information identification process in much the same way that the Service manages the process for a promotion board for the grades of O-7 and O-8. The Services initiate checks for adverse and reportable information from EEO/MEO, Service, and DoD OIG files (the Service IG checks with the DoD OIG); criminal files; and personnel files (for reportable information).

If no adverse information is identified, the military department secretary recommends the officer for the Service position or nominates the officer for the joint position. Once the Secretary of Defense approves an officer for an assignment (Service or joint) the military department secretary will submit a nomination package on the officer. If the officer has adverse or reportable information, that information must be included as part of the nomination package.

Officers nominated to O-9 and O-10 positions are subject to special reviewing requirements specified in the Joint Ethics Regulation.[39] The regulation requires the military department secretary to ensure that the annual personal financial disclosure information in the officer's Office of Government Ethics Form 278 is current and that the Designated Agency Ethics Official or designee has reviewed that financial information relative to the position under consideration. The military department secretaries must also certify that a review has been conducted of "all relevant systems of records maintained by their departments, including investigative files, to determine if there is any evidence that the nominee has violated the rules or standards of conduct," and the secretaries must report whether that review disclosed any violation.[40]

---

[38] CJCSI 1331.01D, *Manpower and Personnel Actions Involving General and Flag Officers*, Washington, D.C.: Joint Chiefs of Staff, August 1, 2010, certified current as of February 11, 2013, pp. E6–E7.

[39] DoDD 5500.07-R, *Joint Ethics Regulation (JER)*, Washington, D.C.: U.S. Department of Defense, August 30, 1993, Incorporating Change 7, November 11, 2011.

[40] DoDD 5500.07-R, August 30, 1993, Incorporating Change 7, November 11, 2011.

Figure 4.3
Personnel Process for Nominations to O-9 and O-10

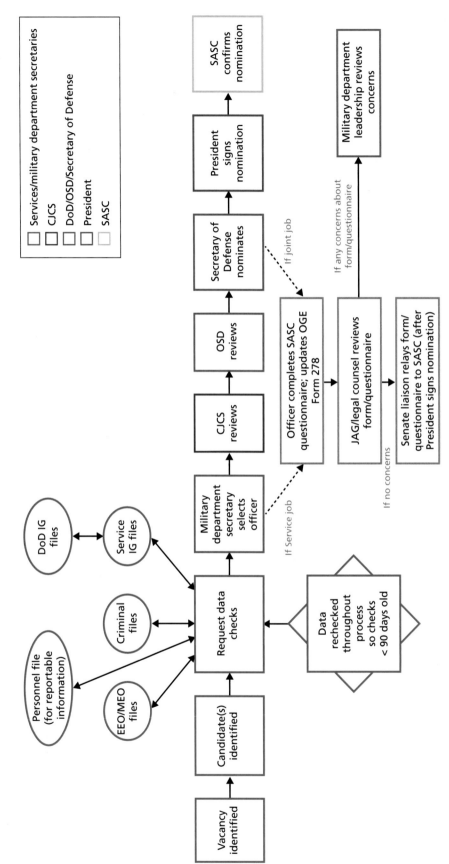

SOURCE: Adapted from Harrell and Hix, 2012, and updated to reflect DoDI 1320.04, 2014.
NOTE: OGE = Office of Government Ethics.

For O-9 and O-10 positions, after the military department secretary has selected the nominee, the officer is also required to complete a SASC questionnaire. If the officer is selected for a joint position, the CJCS review of the candidate's materials occurs while the candidate is completing the SASC questionnaire. The CJCS does not have the opportunity to review the officer's SASC questionnaire before signing off and thus could be caught unaware if within it the officer self-reports any misconduct or allegations against them not otherwise noted in the package. In all cases, the SASC questionnaire is reviewed by the JAG or legal counsel. If the questionnaire raises any concerns, the officer's Service leadership will review it. If no concerns are raised by the SASC questionnaire, the SASC liaison will relay the documents to the SASC once the President has signed off on the nomination.

When the military department secretary has selected a nominee for a position, they submit a nomination memorandum to the CJCS. As outlined in CJCSI 1331.01D (2010), the military department secretary is required to provide information regarding the officer's experience in combat or contingency operations. The policy includes a sample nomination memorandum that includes the following paragraph:

> All systems of records, to include Equal Employment Opportunity files and the Standard Form 278 (Public Financial Disclosure Report), maintained in the Department of Defense that pertain to this officer have been examined. The files contain no adverse information about this officer since his last Senate confirmation. Further, to the best of our knowledge, there is no planned or ongoing investigation or inquiry into matters that constitute alleged adverse information on the part of this officer. Further, Major General Public has not been implicated, nor is there any likelihood that he will be implicated in the Abu [Ghraib] prison abuse scandal.[41]

The nomination package information required by the CJCS for officers nominated to O-9 and O-10 positions differs slightly from the information required for officers nominated to O-7 and O-8 positions. The required elements listed in the 2010 policy are

1. nomination memorandum signed by the military department secretary and, as a courtesy, the Service Chief
2. a current DoD OIG check, not more than 90 days old, with a certification of any connection to Abu Ghraib or detainee operations
3. draft Secretary of Defense memorandum to the President
4. White House scroll
5. biography (both summary and full biography) and joint service summary
6. press release
7. photograph, 8 by 10 inches, glossy[42]

---

[41] CJCSI 1331.01D, 2010, pp. D-A-1–D-A-2. CJCSI 1331-01D, 2010, refers to Standard Form 278, but DoDI 1320.04, 2014, references the current form, which is the Office of Government Ethics Form 278.

[42] G/FO Matters informed us that this photograph is no longer required, because the biography already includes a smaller photograph. More recently, a new memorandum from Secretary of Defense Mark Esper now prohibits the use of photographs in the promotion board and selection processes as an initiative to address diversity, inclusion, and equal opportunity in the military (Mark T. Esper, "Immediate Actions to Address Diversity, Inclusion, and Equal Opportunity in the Military Services," memorandum for Chief Management Officer of the Department of Defense et al., Washington, D.C.: U.S. Department of Defense, July 14, 2020).

8.   adverse information cover sheets, if applicable
9.   time-in-position information.[43]

The CJCS then prepares a memorandum for the nomination package before the package proceeds to OUSD(P&R) for review. For an initial appointment to O-9 or O-10, the CJCS evaluates the officer's joint duty experience.

Retirement from General and Flag Officer Ranks

The 2014 revisions to DoDI 1320.04 expanded the scope of the DoDI to include the retirement process in its guidance for G/FO management. The previous DoDI (1320.4) did not include a reference to the retirement process; however, previous guidance from the Secretary of Defense and the USD(P&R) governed the retirement policy for G/FOs. The O-7 and O-8 retirement process was subject to a 1998 Secretary of Defense memorandum, "Processing Retirement Applications of Officers in the Grades of O-7 and O-8."[44] The O-9 and O-10 retirement process was subject to a 1996 USD(P&R) memorandum, "Memorandum Provides Instructions for the Processing of Three- and Four-Star Retirement Recommendations."[45] DoDI 1320.04 therefore consolidated the guidance previously provided in DoDI 1320.4 and the two memoranda.

The 2010 RAND evaluation noted that both DoD and the SASC focused primarily on the assignment and promotion processes rather than the retirement process. The authors noted that the focus was appropriate, given that the retirement process considers the adverse and reportable information occurring only at the officer's current pay grade and that the retirement process did not require Senate confirmation.[46]

Figure 4.4 depicts the process by which the Services conduct checks for officers retiring from grades O-7 through O-10. The process is the same for all officers retiring from the G/FO ranks through the grade determination process. The process begins once an officer indicates an intent to retire, at which point the Service initiates data checks similar to those required for promotion. If any reportable information is uncovered during this process, the military department secretary determines whether to hold an individual's retirement request until findings become available. The individual is offered the chance to respond to any adverse information. If the adverse information is substantiated, the military department secretary is responsible for making a grade determination for retirement. At this point, the process diverges for officers retiring from the grades of O-7 and O-8 and those retiring from the grades of O-9 and O-10.

As stipulated in Title 10, all commissioned officers, meeting time-in-grade requirements, retire in the highest grade in which they served satisfactorily. If an officer is under investigation for alleged misconduct at the time of retirement, the military department secretary has the authority to conditionally determine the highest grade of satisfactory service while the inves-

[43]   CJCSI 1331.01D, 2010, pp. D-5–D-6.

[44]   Secretary of Defense, "Processing Retirement Applications of Officers in the Grades of O-7 and O-8," memorandum for Secretary of the Army, Secretary of the Navy, Secretary of the Air Force, Under Secretary of Defense (Personnel and Readiness), General Counsel (DoD), and Inspector General (DoD), Washington, D.C., October 9, 1998b.

[45]   OUSD(P&R), "Memorandum Provides Instructions for the Processing of Three- and Four-Star Retirement Recommendations," memorandum for Secretary of the Army, Secretary of the Navy, Secretary of the Air Force, and Chairman of the Joint Chiefs of Staff, Washington, D.C., June 21, 1996.

[46]   Harrell and Hix, 2012, p. 43.

Figure 4.4
Personnel Process for Retirement from General and Flag Officer Ranks

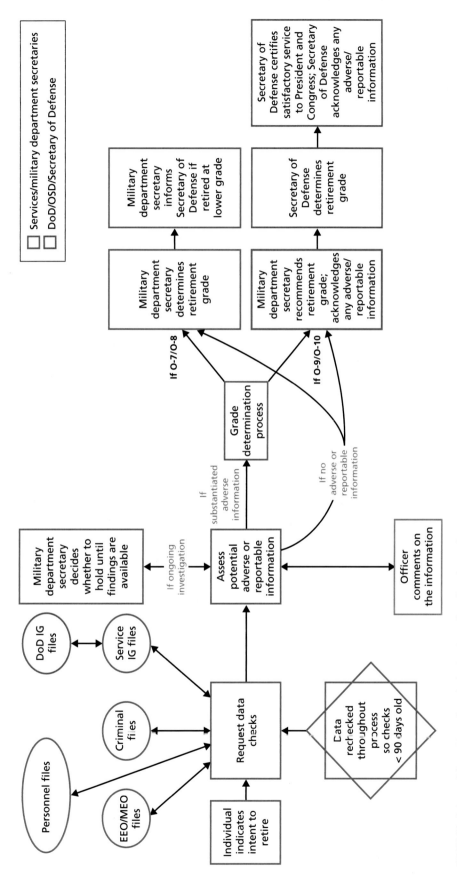

SOURCE: Adapted from Harrell and Hix, 2012, and updated to reflect DoDI 1320.04, 2014.

tigation is pending and allow the officer to retire.[47] Thus, in cases in which the outcomes of investigations are unknown, the officers and their families can be permitted to move forward and to access retirement benefits rather than waiting months or even years for the investigations to conclude. If an investigation results in adverse findings, the officer is retired under a lower grade, and the retired pay is therefore recalculated to the lower grade.[48] In some cases, the certification of an officer's retirement grade may be reopened—particularly if "substantial evidence comes to light after the retirement that could have led to a lower retired grade under this section if known by competent authority at the time of retirement."[49]

Retirement from O-7 and O-8 Grades

With respect to retirement of officers in grades O-7 and O-8, DoDI 1320.04 added new requirements that officers may not be approved for retirement until their names have been checked for adverse and reportable information in DoD, Service, and State IG files and EEO/MEO, NCIC,[50] the Central Clearance Facility, JAG, GC, and other Service database files within the past 90 days.[51] The military department secretary has the authority to approve retirements of officers in the grades of O-7 or O-8. In the event of adverse information, the military department secretary has the authority to permit or deny the officer's retirement in the grade. In the event of pending or ongoing investigations, they have the authority to delay the determination. The military department secretary must request an expedited investigation if possible and appropriate. Furthermore, they have the authority to determine whether a retirement should be approved or delayed if it appears that the investigation will not be completed by the requested date of retirement. They must then report any retirement approval for an officer under investigation to the Secretary of Defense.

Retirement from O-9 and O-10 Grades

For officers retiring in the grades of O-9 and O-10, the secretary of the officer's military department processes the recommendation for retirement through CJCS to the USD(P&R). If there is no adverse or reportable information and no need for a minimum service-in-grade waiver, the USD(P&R) or Deputy USD(P&R) is the approval authority for an officer's retirement.

If the officer's file includes adverse or reportable information added since the Senate confirmation for the grade in which retirement is expected, the Secretary of Defense must determine whether the officer completed either "satisfactory or non-satisfactory service" in the requested retirement grade.[52] The military department secretary must provide the Secretary of Defense with copies of all relevant documentation of any disciplinary action against the officer and provide an affirmative statement in support of the officer's retirement in the grade.[53]

---

[47] This new conditional retirement option was recently added to Title 10 through Sec. 509 of the FY 2019 NDAA (Public Law 115-232, John S. McCain National Defense Authorization Act for Fiscal Year 2019, August 13, 2018).

[48] 10 U.S.C. 1370 (a)(1) and (d)(1).

[49] 10 U.S.C. 1370 (f)(2).

[50] As addressed in Chapter Five, the FBI has since clarified that the NCIC is not permitted to be used as a source of employment information.

[51] DoDI 1320.04, 2014, Enclosure 2, p. 25. See Chapter Five for a discussion of these data sources.

[52] DoDI 1320.04, 2014, p. 22.

[53] DoDI 1320.04, 2014, p. 23.

In cases in which alleged adverse information is identified either while the retirement package is being processed or after a retirement has been announced, the military department secretary or the DoD OIG must notify the USD(P&R) within five duty days. Once such information is identified, G/FO Matters will hold the retirement nomination in abeyance pending review. If the alleged adverse information is substantiated, the military department secretary must resubmit the retirement package for Secretary of Defense consideration.[54]

The Secretary of Defense or the USD(P&R) approves the retirement, at which point G/FO Matters submits certifications of satisfactory service to the President and (24 hours later) to the president of the Senate and the Speaker of the House of Representatives. After the President and congressional leadership have been notified, G/FO Matters sends copies of the certifications to the military department secretary. At this point, the retirement may be publicly announced.

As noted in the previous section on O-7 and O-8 retirements, the FY 2019 NDAA authorization for conditional retirement enables officers with an ongoing investigation to retire while retaining the option to reopen the retirement pay grade determination process should the allegation be substantiated or other misconduct revealed.[55]

Interactions Between Offices

The personnel processes outlined in this chapter require working relationships between the offices involved, including G/FO Matters, Service G/FO management offices, DoD and Service IGs, JAs, and GCs. These offices must coordinate notifications, status updates, and requests for information. The processes also benefit by the offices sharing information through training, guidance, and advice on applying policy. Although not an explicit focus of our study, the need for strong working relationships across offices was repeatedly brought up in interviews with Service and DoD representatives. Some of the civilian professionals have held positions in these offices for many years and have built up these relationships and institutional knowledge to draw upon. The success of these processes depends in part upon individuals cooperating across many different organizations to implement the law and the policy, and thus such relationships will be important to preserve.

Summary

The 2014 policy update in DoDI 1320.04 laid out the various personnel action processes according to various grades. In addition, it expanded responsibility for ensuring compliance from a single office in DoD to a shared responsibility across USD(P&R), the secretaries of the military departments, and the CJCS. As a result, interaction with officer personnel packages has increased at these senior levels. The new policy also included retirement packages in the scope of personnel actions that required a review of any reportable and adverse information.

The relevant personnel processes that consider adverse information include the appointment and promotion processes for officers in pay grades O-4 and above in the active com-

---

[54] DoDI 1320.04, 2014, pp. 24–25.

[55] Pub. L. 115-232, 2018.

ponent and O-6 and above in the reserve component. Adverse *and* reportable information is considered in the board processes for officers for the O-7 and O-8 pay grades, the assignment and promotion nomination processes for O-9 and O-10 grades, and the G/FO retirement process. Adverse and reportable information is also required to be included in O-2 and O-3 active packages and O-2 through O-5 reserve packages when that information has received significant media attention or is an item of interest to the SASC. The policy does not include any requirements regarding the retirement for officers in the pay grades below G/FO ranks. Although DoDI 1320.04 outlines the process for appointment, promotion, and retirement, it does not integrate DoD guidance regarding cross-Service or cross-component transfers. New requirements for O-6-and-below adverse and reportable information processes laid forth in DoDI 1320.04 continue to evolve, particularly regarding the update to Title 10 now requiring the Services to furnish adverse information to all boards considering officer promotions to O-4, O-5, and O-6 for active-component officers and to O-6 for reserve-component officers.

For O-7 to O-10 officers and for those being promoted to O-7, the Services are required to check IG, EEO/MEO, the Central Clearance Facility, legal, and criminal justice files for potentially adverse or reportable information. This process is completed before a package is submitted to G/FO Matters and before it is provided to the White House and the Senate, and these data checks are required to remain updated until the promotion or nomination is confirmed by the Senate.

Although there are common elements in the process across pay grades, some differences exist by pay grade. For promotions to the grade of O-7, officers do not have to complete a financial disclosure, while officers nominated for appointment to the grades of O-8 through O-10 must submit one. Service promotion boards select officers for promotion to the grades of O-7 and O-8, but officers appointed to the grades of O-9 and O-10 are selected by the military department secretary and reviewed by the CJCS and USD(P&R) before the Secretary of Defense recommends that the President nominate the officer. Appointments to the grades of O-9 and O-10 are *positional*, meaning that individuals are promoted to the rank associated with the position to which they are nominated. Therefore, those officers can remain in the same grade by filling sequential positions associated with that grade.

Retirement processes for G/FOs are conducted similarly in each Service and vary from other personnel processes. These processes focus on adverse information from only the current pay grade of a retiring officer and do not require Senate confirmation. A recent development is that Congress now authorizes an officer with an ongoing investigation to be conditionally retired, which provides the option to revisit the retirement pay grade determination should the allegation be substantiated or other misconduct revealed.

CHAPTER FIVE
Sources of Adverse and Reportable Information

Chapter Four indicated when in a process the Services and DoD must consult different sources to identify any potential adverse or reportable information regarding the officers under consideration. These information sources document complaints, investigations, or actions taken against individuals for inappropriate or undesirable behavior. There is no single organization or database with a unified set of all potential types of negative information the Services or DoD might possess about an officer. Different organizations have different authorities and responsibilities. Therefore, multiple sources belonging to multiple organizations must be searched. Any potentially unfavorable information meeting the definitions of adverse or reportable information must be assessed before the Services and DoD can certify an officer as demonstrating exemplary conduct in support of a positive personnel action, such as a promotion.

This chapter describes those potential sources of adverse and reportable information that DoD policy states must be checked prior to forwarding any G/FO personnel action for DoD or Presidential approval or Senate confirmation.[1] More specifically, the sources named in DoDI 1320.04 are DoD, Service, and state IG; EEO; EO; NCIC; Central Clearance Facility; and JAG and GC records. This chapter also discusses command-directed investigation (CDI) files,[2] which are not explicitly named in this policy but could fall under the policy's category of "other Service database files."[3] As discussed in Chapter Four, a search of each of these information sources is not mandated by DoD for personnel actions for the much larger O-6-and-below officer populations. Personnel action package requirements vary by pay grade groups, with increasing scrutiny applied to the officers chosen for the G/FO ranks, which have the highest officer levels of authority and responsibility. Still, these information sources can assist the military department secretaries in determining whether officers meet the exemplary conduct standard, which does apply to officers across the ranks.

For each of these information sources, we provide an overview of the types of adverse and reportable information covered; where that information comes from; and any strengths, limitations, or issues with the source's records or search tools, as characterized by the offices that conduct or review products from these data checks. In this chapter, we pay greater attention to organizations that conduct the investigations and generate the investigation reports than to the offices that review others' investigation documents and provide legal evaluations and counsel

---

[1] DoDI 1320.04, 2014, p. 19.

[2] These are also referred to as *commander-directed investigations*, *AR 15-6 investigations* (Army), and *JAGMAN investigations* (Navy and Marine Corps).

[3] DoDI 1320.04, 2014, p. 19.

(JAG and GC). For more-comprehensive descriptions of how information is obtained, recorded, tracked, and reported and for other details, we provide references to applicable policies.

This chapter also provides examples of information sources not explicitly listed in DoDI 1320.04 as sources to be checked but that could hold unfavorable information that might surface later and have implications for the approval or confirmation of a proposed personnel action. Some of these sources might fall under the "other Service database files" portion of the required data checks, specifically professional license complaint information and information pertaining to the civilian employment record of reserve-component personnel who are also Service or DoD employees. As we will discuss in this chapter, it is not feasible or practical to check every possible military and civilian information source for adverse and reportable information; however, there might be additional sources that the Services or DoD have access to that might be worth the resources and time to systematically address for a subset of packages, if not for all of them.

U.S. Department of Defense, Service, and State Inspector General Records

Types and Sources of Adverse and Reportable Information

Congress established the DoD OIG to serve as an independent and objective unit within DoD.[4] The head of the DoD OIG is a civilian appointed by the President and confirmed by the Senate. The mission of this organization is as follows:

- To detect and deter fraud, waste, and abuse in Department of Defense programs and operations;
- Promote the economy, efficiency, and effectiveness of the DoD; and
- Help ensure ethical conduct throughout the DoD.[5]

The DoD OIG's numerous responsibilities include advising the Secretary of Defense on audit and criminal investigative matters and on the prevention and detection of fraud, waste, and abuse in programs and operations of DoD. Specific examples of the types of violations within the scope of the DoD OIG include inappropriate relationships; failure to follow regulations; computer crimes; leaks of classified information; whistleblower reprisals; bribery; sex trafficking; contract and procurement fraud; government travel fraud; and misuse of a government vehicle, equipment, or facilities.

In addition to initiating and conducting its own audits, investigations, evaluations, and inspections, the DoD OIG is responsible for supervising and coordinating those activities within DoD, including the IGs of the Joint Staff, Combatant Commands, and Services. The DoD OIG is responsible for providing policy and direction to other organizations within DoD

---

[4]   See the Inspector General Act of 1978, as amended, in 5 U.S.C. Appendix. An overarching DoD OIG policy (DoDD 5106.01) describes the mission, organization and management, responsibilities and functions, relationships, and authorities of the DoD OIG, as authorized by law (DoDD 5106.01, *Inspector General of the Department of Defense*, April 20, 2012, Incorporating Change 1, August 19, 2014, written in accordance with 10 U.S.C. 113, 10 U.S.C. 141, and 5 U.S.C. Appendix). This policy has been updated since our review (now Incorporating Change 2, May 29, 2020).

[5]   DoD OIG, "Our Mission," webpage, undated.

responsible for such audits, investigations, evaluations, and inspections,[6] as well as monitoring and evaluating their work. The DoD OIG has the authority to access all records available to any DoD component (e.g., reports, investigations, recommendations).

Service policies also guide the Service IGs on Service-specific procedures for meeting DoD and Service requirements. For National Guard personnel working for their states (under Title 32 authority) rather than in their federal capacity (under Title 10), active-component Command IGs are assigned to each state and report directly to the adjutant general of that state and the Chief of the National Guard Bureau.[7]

DoD OIG records include information obtained through multiple pathways:

- information that the DoD OIG requested or accessed as part of its audit, evaluation, and inspection functions.
- allegations reported directly to the DoD OIG by a complainant, such as those submitted through the DoD Hotline. Not all of these may fall within the DoD OIG's scope; for example, the DoD OIG might defer action on a complaint if the complainant has submitted the same complaint to another agency with relevant processes, such as a Service or DoD EEO entity for EEO-related issues.
- complaints first received by other individuals or organizations that were subsequently referred to the DoD OIG. As an example that is particularly relevant to our report, DoD OIG regulations require that the DoD OIG be notified of all complaints made about senior officials, and it reserves the right to decide whether it conducts an investigation.[8] The DoD OIG's Directorate for Investigations of Senior Officials is responsible for all of the IG investigations of senior officials. The DoD OIG conducts most of the investigations of O-9 and O-10 officers. It delegates more investigations of officers who are O-7 selects and O-7 and O-8 officers to subordinate IGs, although the DoD OIG will provide oversight of investigations conducted by others and will thus have records of those, except for investigations of allegations of reprisal, which are handled by the Whistleblower Reprisal Investigations Directorate—which also investigates sexual assault–related reprisal cases.

DoDI 1320.04 mandates that, for personnel actions for pay grades O-7 through O-10, checks of DoD IG records for adverse or reportable information be kept current (not more than 90 days old). The initial screening is required to occur at both the military department level and the DoD OIG level. Then, the military departments are required to ensure that the Service IG and DoD OIG information forwarded to G/FO Matters is kept current throughout

---

[6] Examples of such DoD OIG Instructions include DoDI 5505.07, 2018; and DoDI 5505.16, *Investigations by DoD Components*, Washington, D.C.: U.S. Department of Defense, June 23, 2017.

[7] National Guard, "Inspector General (NGB-IG)," webpage, undated.

[8] DoDD 5505.06, *Investigations of Allegations of Senior DoD Officials*, Washington, D.C.: U.S. Department of Defense, June 6, 2013. The term *senior official* includes current and retired G/FOs, officers selected for promotion to O-7 and included in the promotion board report submitted to the military department secretary, and civilian senior leaders not within the scope of this study. Overviews of DoD OIG senior official investigations have been reported in periodic reports to the Congress (e.g., DoD OIG, *Semiannual Report to the Congress*, Alexandria, Va: U.S. Department of Defense, October 1, 2019–March 31, 2020.)

the personnel action process (whether the package is with DoD, the President, or the Senate) and that DoD is notified of any new or newly discovered adverse or reportable information.[9]

Strengths, Limitations, and Issues

There are numerous strengths to the IGs' roles in collecting, tracking, and reporting adverse and reportable information involving military officers. The scope of IG investigations spans a variety of problematic behaviors relevant for decisionmakers determining whether officers demonstrate exemplary conduct. The IG role is to serve as an independent investigator who focuses on finding and documenting the facts of the matter; IGs do not make decisions or recommendations about whether any corrective or punitive actions should be taken. IG investigations are recorded and tracked in electronic databases. In circumstances in which the DoD, Joint Staff, Combatant Command, and Service IGs refer out-of-scope complaints to commanders for possible administrative investigation, the IGs then track the progress and outcomes of any resulting CDIs. It is within IG responsibilities to review whether commanders took appropriate action according to the law or policy related to the particular offense.

The management and tracking of all senior-official investigations is centralized within the DoD OIG. The IG tracking of officers who are not senior officials is not as complete or centralized. The Service IGs are all working within their own respective databases rather than from a unified IG database. The DoD OIG is working to expand and enhance the use of its database for use by the Service IGs. Service IG checks for adverse or reportable information might miss investigations conducted by another Service, as might be the case on joint bases or in deployed environments. The representatives we met with explained that Service IGs sometimes do share that information with one another, such as when they are located together in a joint environment, but there are no formal policy requirements that all Service IGs send a notification to the other Services, nor do they check with other Service IGs when adverse and reportable information checks are conducted. We note that such additional requirements would increase the Service IG workload. If the Joint Staff IG receives an allegation about a current member of the Joint Staff, it will notify the relevant Combatant Command IG and Service IG. For senior officials, the Joint Staff IG will also notify the DoD OIG.

Also regarding officers in pay grades O-6 and below,[10] the IGs typically track only the CDIs that began as complaints to them and were then referred to commanders rather than all CDIs. Thus, the IG databases are only a partial record of CDIs, because these databases are not intended to be a central repository for CDIs. A notable exception is the Air Force, which since 2018 has required that all commanders notify their IGs as soon as a CDI or other inquiry involving an officer is initiated.[11] This process provides the Air Force with a fuller record for determining whether officers selected for promotion or appointment are fully qualified and

---

[9] DoDI 1320.04, 2014, Enclosure 5.

[10] This excludes those who are included in the category of senior officials because they have been selected for promotion to O-7 and included in the promotion board report submitted to the military department secretary.

[11] This was initiated by a memorandum (Assistant Secretary of the Air Force for Manpower and Reserve Affairs, *Policy Change—Requirement for Commanders to Report Initiation of Commander Directed Investigations (CDI) or Inquiry to the Local IG for All Officers Below the Grade of Brigadier General*, memorandum for all commanders, July 5, 2018) and subsequently incorporated into an Air Force Instruction (AFI 90-301, *Inspector General Complaints Resolution*, Washington, D.C.: Department of the Air Force, December 28, 2018).

meet the exemplary conduct provisions of 10 U.S.C. 8583.[12] This process also helps the Air Force cover the information gap on new investigations after a commander recommends an officer for promotion and before the officer's personnel action package is approved, and it provides a longer-term CDI record accessible at the headquarters level that could be accessed for future personnel actions. The Army diverges from all other IG processes in a different way: by instructing its IGs to delete the officer's name from the searchable subject/suspect fields in their IG database when closing out a case once the CDI has been completed.[13] The Army concern was that substantiated allegations from a CDI would appear in an IG records name search for some officers (if the complaint was first reported to the IG) and not for others (if the complaint was first reported to the chain of command). Recent Army policy revisions state that Army IGs will record these CDI cases first reported to the IG as "command referred" rather than "substantiated" or "not substantiated," which is relevant because substantiated allegations might meet the further definition of *adverse information*.[14] There is an instruction to note the complainant's name before removing CDI products from the database, but there is no note to similarly retain the subject's name. Thus, whereas the Air Force policy addresses this disparity across officers by requiring the IG to track in a discoverable form the subjects and outcomes of all CDIs, the Army's strategy is to remove the partial CDI information that the IGs have. The Service IGs may differ in their Service-specific regulations, but the Joint Staff IG follows the DoD OIG training and guidance, meaning that if the Joint Staff IG receives a complaint and then refers the issue to a commander for investigation, it tracks and records the progress and outcome of that complaint.

For personnel action packages for officers with adverse or reportable information, the SASC requires that complete, unredacted investigation files, including exhibits and submitted statements, be included for its review before confirmation. The IGs who must provide this type of information also have obligations to protect whistleblowers and to preserve the integrity of their in-progress investigations and the IG system that relies upon individuals to report violations and cooperate with investigators. The IGs also have an obligation to comply with the Privacy Act of 1974. It appears from our interviews that some discussion and further guidance are needed on how best to meet expectations for information-sharing while protecting the identity of whistleblowers, victims, and witnesses and avoiding compromising investigations that have

---

[12] The exemplary conduct provisions are as follows:

All commanding officers and others in authority in the Air Force are required—
(1) to show in themselves a good example of virtue, honor, patriotism, and subordination;
(2) to be vigilant in inspecting the conduct of all persons who are placed under their command;
(3) to guard against and suppress all dissolute and immoral practices, and to correct, according to the laws and regulations of the Air Force, all persons who are guilty of them; and
(4) to take all necessary and proper measures, under the laws, regulations, and customs of the Air Force, to promote and safeguard the morale, the physical well-being, and the general welfare of the officers and enlisted persons under their command or charge. (10 U.S.C. 8583)

[13] The Army Inspector General's *Assistance and Investigations Guide* lists "[r]emove the name of the subject/suspect from the subject/suspect field" as one of the actions required to close a CDI case in the IG database (Army Inspector General, *The Assistance and Investigations Guide*, Fort Belvoir, Va.: Department of the Army Inspector General Agency Training Division, March 2020, p. II-3-6). The Army IG's cover letter states that the guide is authoritative doctrine for all IGs and that it has the backing of Army Regulation (AR) 20-1, *Inspector General Activities and Procedures*, Washington, D.C.: Department of the Army, March 23, 2020.

[14] AR 20-1, 2020, pp. 59–60.

not yet been completed. Additionally, records of in-progress investigations could lead to false conclusions because key interviews or other evidence might at that point be missing.

IG workload and available personnel are also a concern for IGs to be able to complete investigations in a timely manner.[15] In 2018, the DoD OIG explained to a House Armed Services Committee (HASC) hearing several factors that limited the abilities of the IGs (DoD, Service, Joint Command/Combatant Command, and defense agencies) to complete timely investigations.[16] The IGs have had to process an increasing number of complaints. For example, in FY 2008, there were 395 misconduct complaints against senior officials (military or civilian); this number had risen to 815 by FY 2012, and it remained elevated across the five subsequent fiscal years, ranging from a low of 703 to a high of 837.[17] Furthermore, the IGs are investigating increasingly complex matters, including those resulting from a proliferation of digital and electronic evidence. Increased scrutiny of IG reports has led to lengthier and more-detailed documents, which are more labor-intensive to produce. The DoD IG reported that, for many IGs, the increase in caseload and oversight responsibilities has not been supported through budget increases. Thus, in some cases, the timeline to complete investigations has suffered. For example, in FY 2017, the average number of days to complete an IG investigation of an allegation against a senior official (military or civilian) was 147 in the Joint Staff and Combatant Commands, 203 in the Air Force, 223 in the Navy, 321 in the Marine Corps, 453 in the Army, and 472 in the DoD OIG. [18] Extended investigation timelines have implications for officers' careers and military readiness because pending investigations can stop or delay personnel actions, such as appointments, promotions, and retirements.

A final point relates to the section of DoDI 1320.04's *reportable information* definition that states that this reportable information includes "[i]nformation related to alleged misconduct or impropriety, which is subject to an on-going investigative, administrative, or judicial process."[19] When the IGs receive a complaint, there is an initial intake period, prior to formally opening an investigation, in which the offices assess the complaint. For example, the IG will determine whether the allegation is credible, whether it is frivolous, whether it is a duplicate of a complaint already on record, or whether the issue falls within the IG's scope or should be referred to another organization. According to those we interviewed in Service offices involved in the personnel action processes, the IGs use various terms to describe this intake phase, such as *credibility determination*, *evaluation*, and *pre-investigation*. However, there has been some question of whether that stage is actually a reportable open *investigation*, even if the IGs are engaged in fact-finding, because the IG reserves the term *investigation* for a more formal process that might not even follow. Service representatives reported that this pre-investigation activity could take days, weeks, or longer if there are personnel shortages. This issue points not only to ambiguity in the definition of reportable information but also potentially to a

---

[15]   DoD OIG, *Task Force to Improve Timeliness of Senior Officer Administrative Investigations (Redacted)*, Alexandria, Va: U.S. Department of Defense, DoDIG-2015-030, November 4, 2014.

[16]   Glenn A. Fine, "Senior Leader Misconduct: Prevention and Accountability," statement presented before the Subcommittee on Military Personnel, House Armed Services Committee, U.S. House of Representatives, Washington, D.C., February 7, 2018.

[17]   Fine, 2018, p. 7. Note that this rise refers to complaints, since this paragraph is about IG workload: The number of substantiated allegations in this same period declined.

[18]   Fine, 2018, p. 14.

[19]   DoDI 1320.04, 2014, p. 16.

delay in reporting or a lack of reporting information that the Senate would expect to receive. SASC professional staff explained that for nomination packages already received, the Senate expects to be notified as soon as a complaint is received, not after preliminary fact-finding has already been underway. For G/FOs, DoDI 1320.04 is clear that if the military department or the DoD OIG "identifies any adverse information, pending alleged adverse information, reportable information, or an investigation not previously reported on an officer being recommended for a military officer personnel action," then, "[i]n those cases where the nomination has already reached the White House or Senate, the Secretary of the military department will immediately notify OEPM."[20] OEPM manages the hold and restart processes, which include notifications that need to be sent to the White House or the SASC.

Equal Employment Opportunity Records

Types and Sources of Adverse and Reportable Information

Military officers may lead civilian employees who work for the military, as well as military service members. In DoD, the term *equal employment opportunity* refers to the opportunities for its civilian employees, while the terms *equal opportunity* and *military equal opportunity* apply to the opportunities for military service members.[21] This distinction is important because the laws, policies, and processes for managing complaints from federal employees are quite different from those that apply to service members. This section addresses EEO-related sources of adverse and reportable information, and the next section addresses MEO-related sources.

External to DoD, the U.S. Equal Employment Opportunity Commission (EEOC) is an "independent federal agency that promotes equal opportunity employment through administrative and judicial enforcement of the federal civil rights laws."[22] Because the EEOC has jurisdiction over civilian charges of discrimination against employers, cases involving EEO discrimination are processed outside DoD.

In terms of military officer information that might be adverse or reportable, the DoD civilian EEO program addresses employment discrimination related to a variety of statuses. EEO

> [p]rohibits unlawful employment discrimination based on race, sex (including pregnancy, gender identity, and sexual orientation when based on sex stereotyping), color, national origin, age, religion, disability, genetic information, or reprisal for previous EEO activity in accordance with applicable statutes and [U.S.] Equal Employment Opportunity Commission (EEOC) regulations. While not enforced by the EEOC, discrimination in employment based on other factors prohibited by Executive order, such as status as a parent, may be addressed through other separate complaint and resolution systems.[23]

---

[20] DoDI 1320.04, 2014, pp. 20–21.

[21] The distinction is described in the overarching policy, DoDD 1020.02E, *Diversity Management and Equal Opportunity in the DoD*, Washington, D.C.: U.S. Department of Defense, June 8, 2015, Incorporating Change 2, June 1, 2018. The EEO policy was last updated more than 25 years ago: DoDD 1440.1, *The DoD Civilian Equal Employment Opportunity (EEO) Program*, Washington, D.C.: U.S. Department of Defense, May 21, 1987, Administrative Reissuance Incorporating Through Change 3, April 17, 1992.

[22] U.S. Department of Labor, "Equal Employment Opportunity," webpage, undated.

[23] DoDD 1020.02E, 2015, Incorporating Change 2, 2018, p. 7.

Representatives from the Services and the Diversity Management Operations Center discussed with us examples of the types of EEO complaints that involve military officers. These include civilian employee complaints regarding nonselection for positions, performance evaluations, harassment (with nonsexual more common than sexual), a hostile work environment tied to a protected class, and disciplinary actions perceived to be unfair in comparison with others.

The federal sector EEO complaint process, outlined on the EEOC website and discussed in interviews we conducted,[24] involves many sequential steps, some of which must occur within a specified time frame. The employee typically has 45 days after the discriminatory matter to bring a complaint to the local Service EEO office. In the initial intake phase, the local EEO office enters the complaint into its iComplaints[25] case management software database as an "informal complaint" and tracks the case by the complainant's name and the docket number. This complaint could be lodged against a single individual, such as a supervisor or a commander, or against all military members and civilian employees in the employee's chain of command, up through to the military department secretary or the Secretary of Defense, regardless of whether each of these individuals had any direct role in the alleged discriminatory action. EEO representatives explained that complainants do not always provide names, full names, or accurate names in their claims. For example, they might provide the name of the officer's position (e.g., the installation commander) or the rank and the last name (e.g., General Jones). What the complainant reports is what is entered in the description. The local Service EEO counselor will document the alleged responsible management officials (RMOs) as provided by the complainant and determine whether the complaint falls within the scope of EEO discrimination and timeliness for reporting the matter. The EEO counselor will explain the employee's rights and the EEO process and timeline and attempt to reach an informal resolution. If this complaint is not within the EEO scope, the EEO counselor can give the complainant a list of other options for reporting. For EEO matters, the counselor may gather additional facts surrounding the complaint through such methods as speaking with the person(s) alleged to have been discriminatory or others who were present. The initial EEO counseling, fact-finding, and resolution attempt needs to be accomplished within 30 days of the complaint being made, though it can be extended up to 60 days.[26]

The information gathered up to this point is shared with the complainant, and the local Service EEO counselor makes one last effort at informal resolution. The complainant then has 15 days to decide whether they will file a formal complaint. If the employee does file a formal complaint and the Service accepts the formal complaint,[27] the Service EEO office is to send the information within 30 days to DoD's Investigations and Resolution Directorate (IRD) within the Diversity Management Operations Center of Defense Human Resources Activity. That information is transmitted via the Investigations and Resolutions Case Management

---

[24] EEOC, "Overview of Federal Sector EEO Complaint Process," webpage, undated.

[25] The Air Force's EEO, the Air Force Civilian Appellate Review Office, has been working with the Case Management Tracking Analysis and Reporting System as well.

[26] Employees also might have the option to go through alternative dispute resolution, such as mediation, rather than EEO informal counseling.

[27] The Service can dismiss the complaint for a procedural reason (e.g., it was filed more than 45 days after the incident), if the complaint has already been adjudicated, or if it is not under the purview of the EEOC, but the employee has the option to appeal within 30 days of the dismissal.

System (IRCMS). Then, the IRD is supposed to complete an independent investigation within 120 days, because regulations require that the entire process be completed in 180 days, and 30 days before and after the IRD investigation are reserved for Service activity. An investigator is assigned to gather testimonial evidence (via face-to-face or telephone interviews) and conduct other impartial fact-finding to augment the evidence provided by the local Service EEO counselor. All of this information is placed into an investigative file for the case, which includes the report of investigation and all supporting documentation. The IRD conducts all of the EEO investigations for DoD and its components.

The IRD sends this investigative file back to the Service EEO again using the IRCMS software. The Service in turn shares this information with the complainant and makes the employee aware of two options to proceed if there is a preference to continue: pursue a hearing with an EEOC administrative judge who will make a decision based on the preponderance of the evidence, or request a final agency action. The complainant has 30 days to decide between these two options.

If the employee proceeds with an EEOC hearing, the hearing can take two to five years to schedule because of a backlog of EEOC cases,[28] which include complaints from all U.S. organizations, not just those in DoD. In FY 2018, the average time to resolution for a case was 633 days.[29] DoD cases do not receive any national security priority over any other cases.

If the complainant instead requests a final agency action, that decision is supposed to be made within 60 days. Whichever route the employee chooses, the right to appeal the decision leaves open the possibility for more steps and a longer timeline for an open allegation.

Strengths, Limitations, and Issues

Each of the Services has an electronic database system that allows the local installation EEO counselor to transmit case information to the military department–level EEO office. Additionally, a single agency in DoD conducts all of the EEO investigations for OSD and the Services, and thus these investigations are guided by the same policies and processes for that fact-finding requirement. The EEO process gathers and records allegations against officers for certain types of issues that are outside the scope of the IG, and thus searching EEO records complements the data in IG investigation records.

One of the limitations of these EEO records is the ability to search easily for cases involving particular officers. Each of the military departments uses a separate version of a common EEO complaint management software (iComplaints) that helps them track the cases according to the name of the person who made the complaint, not by the name or names of the individual or individuals alleged to have been discriminatory. Because of the limitations of the software, when the EEO offices receive a list of officer names to check in their databases, someone has to manually type each officer's name to search the database. Offices do not have the feature to upload a spreadsheet or a list for a batch search. With common names, further work might be needed to determine whether the person named in the complaint is indeed the officer on the list of names being checked for adverse or reportable information. Additionally, the software will find the name only if the searcher types the name just as the complainant

[28] For more information on the EEOC hearing backlog and efforts to reduce it, see EEOC, "Performance and Accountability Report Fiscal Year 2018," webpage, November 15, 2018; and EEOC OIG, *Draft Report: Evaluation of EEOC Federal Hearings and Appeals Processes*, OIG Report No. 2018-01-EOIG, March 27, 2020.

[29] EEOC OIG, 2020, p. 15.

provided it (e.g., full name versus initials, first name included, or just the rank and last name). Thus, name checks of the EEO database could fail to find a case within its records containing allegations against an officer, and this case could later come to the attention of the Senate and lead to questions about why the Service failed to report it.

Another potential gap in EEO name checks is that the separate EEO offices do not have access to one another's databases. If a Department of the Navy civilian employee files a complaint against an Air Force officer, that complaint will be recorded and tracked in the Department of the Navy EEO office's database but not in the Department of the Air Force's. So, if the Air Force searches only the EEO complaints it is managing, it will not find that complaint against one of its own officers. Representatives from the Service EEO offices said that they do communicate with one another and would share that information, but there would be no parallel tracking of one case in two Services' databases, and, as mentioned, they do not have access to one another's databases.

Also problematic is that an employee who files an EEO complaint could name anyone as the source of the discrimination or an RMO, including officers several levels above the employee who have neither had any interaction with the employee nor made the decision in question. Furthermore, the names provided by the complainant could be incorrect, partial, or missing altogether.

If not resolved early in the process, EEO complaints can take years to resolve. In the context of our study, the implications are that military careers could end while officers whose personnel actions are unable to proceed in the interim are waiting for resolutions. The time it takes to schedule an EEOC hearing is outside DoD's control. We are unaware of any past or current efforts to form an agreement that could prioritize or fast-track DoD cases. In terms of the portion of the process that DoD or the Services do control, a Diversity Management Operations Center representative reported that IRD investigations average about 150 days, thus exceeding the 120-day window. This challenge has been a long-standing issue: A 2015 RAND assessment noted that

> [s]ince at least 2005, 38 percent to 53 percent of EEO complaints filed each year in DoD have not been processed within this regulated 180-day time frame. When complaint processing exceeds 180 days, DoD is in violation of federal regulations and at risk of sanctions from the EEOC for discrimination based on procedural issues, and the employee who filed the complaint may continue to work in a discriminatory environment.[30]

Multiple assessments and initiatives have been undertaken in recent years to streamline the processes for greater efficiency.[31] Thus, the representative from the Diversity Management Operations Center attributed the overrun to the number of staff available to investigate between approximately 2,800 and 3,300 cases every year, with a queue of cases waiting for an investigator to become available.

Another relevant issue is that EEO complaints often result in a settlement agreement with no clear adjudication of culpability or responsibility, making it unclear whether the underlying conduct is reportable. The DoD policy definitions do not specify whether settlement

---

[30] Miriam Matthews and Nelson Lim, *Improving the Timeliness of Equal Employment Opportunity Complaint Processing in Department of Defense*, Santa Monica, Calif.: RAND Corporation, RR-680-OSD, 2015, pp. xi–xii.

[31] For an example, see Matthews and Lim, 2015.

agreements and the associated complaint documents are reportable information or should be excluded.

For those EEO cases that are not settled and move forward to a hearing, judges' final decisions are succinct and state whether there was a finding of discrimination, not who was responsible for what wrongs. The EEO representatives with whom we met reported that few complaints that end up before an EEO judge result in a finding of discrimination. Even cases that reach this stage might not be finished, because the complainant has the right to appeal. Holding officer personnel packages until EEOC allegations are resolved could effectively end many careers over allegations that would not end up being supported by an independent judge's assessment of the evidence. The timely resolution of EEO complaints is such a challenge that, for EEO inquiries that include an officer for pro forma reasons (such as those complaints that name an entire chain of command) or inquiries in which it appears highly unlikely that there will be a finding of discrimination, the SASC has created an exception to the rule about not confirming officers with pending investigations.

Military Equal Opportunity Records

Types and Sources of Adverse and Reportable Information

The 2010 RAND review noted that the previous guidance (as outlined in DoDI 1320.4 and CJCS guidance) was unclear about whether MEO data checks were required for processing nominations. The previous DoD policy, DoDI 1320.4, had stated: "The Secretaries of the military departments shall ensure that all investigative files, to include Equal Employment Opportunity files, are reviewed prior to forwarding a nomination to the Secretary of Defense."[32] Because the RAND assessment had discovered that the policy was intended to include MEO, its report recommended that the policy be revised to mention both MEO and EEO to help ensure understanding that they are different but both relevant.[33] The updated 2014 instruction (DoDI 1320.04) specifically lists MEO, in addition to EEO, as a data source of information that should be checked.

Recall that MEO (sometimes referred to as EO) refers to the program for military personnel rather than the program for civilian employees within DoD.[34] Policy states that DoD's MEO program does the following:

a. Promotes equal opportunity as being critical to mission accomplishment, unit cohesiveness, and military readiness. Evaluates Service members only on individual merit, fitness, capability, and performance.

b. Ensures that . . . All Service members are afforded equal opportunity in an environment free from harassment, including sexual harassment, and unlawful discrimination on

---

[32] DoDI 1320.4, 1995, p. 3.

[33] Harrell and Hix, 2012, p. 35.

[34] The overarching policy encompassing both EEO and MEO is DoDD 1020.02E, 2015. The MEO-specific policy is DoDD 1350.2, *Department of Defense Military Equal Opportunity (MEO) Program*, Washington, D.C.: U.S. Department of Defense, August 18, 1995, certified current as of November 21, 2003, Incorporating Change 2, June 8, 2015. Also highly relevant, because harassment of military personnel is an MEO issue, is DoDI 1020.03, *Harassment Prevention and Response in the Armed Forces*, Washington, D.C.: U.S. Department of Defense, February 8, 2018.

the basis of race, color, national origin, religion, sex (including gender identity), or sexual orientation.[35]

DoD policy related to MEO has undergone significant change since the 2010 RAND review, and the Office of Diversity Management and Equal Opportunity has been reorganized into the Office for Diversity, Equity, and Inclusion. DoDI 1020.03 (2018) provided the most-comprehensive and most-detailed descriptions to date of types of prohibited harassment behaviors: harassment, discriminatory harassment, sexual harassment, bullying, hazing, retaliation, and reprisal. These behaviors are prohibited regardless of whether the service members are on duty. The new policy clarified that harassment, sexual harassment, bullying, and hazing can occur through electronic communications, as well as in person,[36] and that DoD considers supervisor or commander use or condoning of sexual harassment to be a form of sexual harassment.[37] The new policy also updated the prevention and response policies, programs, and procedures to include options for identifiable and anonymous complaints and "procedures and requirements for responding to, processing, resolving, tracking, and reporting harassment complaints; and training and education requirements and standards."[38]

Consistent with preexisting MEO policy (DoDD 1350.2), DoD's current strategy is to resolve informal complaints at the lowest level possible. Military personnel who believe they have experienced unlawful discrimination can contact the local MEO specialist to have their concern investigated and resolved, or they can report the complaint through a hotline. However, the chain of command is generally the "primary and preferred channel for identifying and correcting discriminatory practices."[39] Although there are Service-specific regulations and methods for addressing incidents of harassment, there are some common elements across them, as required by DoD policy, such as informal and formal complaint systems, timelines for processing complaints, apprising complainants of the status and outcome of the complaints, options for appeal, and documenting the cases.

The first step after receiving a complaint is to determine whether the complaint concerns alleged unlawful discrimination. If it does not, the complainant should be referred to the appropriate agency for that concern. If the complaint includes allegations of sexual assault, it must be referred to a military criminal investigative organization (and to a sexual assault response coordinator for victim support services). If the complaint includes allegations against senior officials (for military officers that means those in pay grades O-7 to O-10 and those being promoted to O-7), it must be reported to the DoD OIG, which will conduct the investigation or assign and oversee it.

---

[35] DoDD 1020.02E, 2015, p. 6.

[36] DoDI 1020.03, 2018, pp. 9–11.

[37] DoDI 1020.03, 2018, p. 9.

[38] DoDI 1020.03, 2018, p. 1. Note that, "[a]lthough the MEO program establishes anti–sexual harassment and anti-discrimination policy for the department, in terms of span of control, it is not resourced to actively oversee service policy compliance and implementation" (Jefferson P. Marquis, Coreen Farris, Kimberly Curry Hall, Kristy N. Kamarck, Nelson Lim, Douglas Shontz, Paul S. Steinberg, Robert Stewart, Thomas E. Trail, Jennie W. Wenger, Anny Wong, and Eunice C. Wong, *Improving Oversight and Coordination of Department of Defense Programs That Address Problematic Behaviors Among Military Personnel*, Santa Monica, Calif.: RAND Corporation, RR-1352-OSD, 2017, p. 80).

[39] DoDD 1350.2, 2015, p. 3.

One option for the complainant is an informal complaint process. This could include addressing the individual directly, asking a coworker to intervene, or requesting that the chain of command resolve it. For informal complaints, the chain of command should initiate a prompt, fair, and impartial CDI to determine whether the complaint can be substantiated. The chain of command should also document the status and outcome of the complaint. If the allegation is substantiated, the commander should take corrective action. In joint environments, the harassment complaints should be processed "through the Command or Service that has administrative control, or disciplinary authority, or a combination thereof, over the alleged offender."[40]

The military complainant also has the option to file a written formal complaint through the MEO office, either initially or as an appeal to the outcome of the informal complaint process. For a formal complaint, the MEO office notifies the unit commander of the complaint and gathers factual information about the complaint.[41] For an unsubstantiated complaint, the JA reviews the report, the unit commander notifies the alleged offender, and the MEO staff briefs the complainant on the outcome. The complainant has the right to appeal the administrative findings to the installation commander or, for complainants not assigned to an installation, to the first commander in the chain with general court-martial convening authority.[42] For a substantiated complaint, the unit commander takes actions to correct the discrimination and advises the MEO office of these actions. The alleged offender has the right to appeal the findings. The MEO office briefs the complainant on its findings and the command's actions. Complainants who believe that reprisal has occurred as a result of either the informal or the formal MEO process are referred to the IG.

Strengths, Limitations, and Issues

DoD policy has become increasingly specific about the types of harassment and discrimination that are not to be tolerated; expectations for prevention efforts; and requirements for complaint processing, accountability, victim support, and documentation of complaints, investigations, findings, and corrective actions. MEO-related investigations can be conducted by different organizations, depending on the nature of the investigation and complainant preference. Investigations may be command-directed or conducted by an MEO specialist or an IG.

Regardless of the complaint process, DoDI 1020.03 requires that the secretaries of the military departments and the other DoD component heads "[m]andate that substantiated complaints are annotated on fitness reports or performance evaluations."[43] We are not aware of any evaluations of the extent to which fitness reports and performance evaluations include information regarding all complaints of harassment that are substantiated through CDIs, IG investigations, or MEO investigations. How swiftly, consistently, thoroughly, and accurately this annotation is being done has implications for military officer personnel actions, because the boards consider fitness reports and performance evaluations when making recommendations for promotions or federal recognition of promotions of military officers.

---

[40] DoDI 1020.03, 2018 p. 15.

[41] DoDI 1020.03, 2018.

[42] DoDD 1350.2, 1995; certified current as of November 21, 2003; Incorporating Change 2, June 8, 2015, p. 10.

[43] DoDI 1020.03, 2018, p. 7.

Currently, the data checks for MEO complaints against officers vary by Service and allow for gaps in reporting. The Army's MEO database was decommissioned in 2019 because of problems related to the technology's age, but its value was limited anyway because it did not include personally identifiable information. For adverse and reportable information checks, the Army will detect an MEO complaint against an officer only if it appears outside the MEO program, such as cases reported to an IG. The Army is exploring the possibility of enhancing the capability of the database for its Sexual Harassment/Assault Response and Prevention program to include additional types of MEO complaints regarding EO, bullying, and hazing. The U.S. Navy had created a centralized MEO database in 2013, but it used this database for only about a year and a half because the system was not meeting its needs; the system was unable to keep pace with evolving DoD MEO policy and expectations. Currently, the headquarters-level data collection and monitoring process begins when a commander's operational report to U.S. Navy headquarters includes an MEO incident. From there, the U.S. Navy MEO office will begin tracking the case manually, through numerous email exchanges requesting details and updates and by recording the information in a spreadsheet. Since mid–FY 2017, the U.S. Navy's MEO office has added identifiable information to the characteristics it is tracking; however, no one contacts that office for data checks on officer adverse and reportable information. The Air Force has a centralized MEO database that is searchable by name, and it began a process of merging its MEO and EEO databases in June 2020.

National Crime Information Center Records

Types and Sources of Adverse and Reportable Information
DoDI 1320.04 specifies that secretaries of the military departments will ensure that NCIC files, along with other listed files, are reviewed for adverse or reportable information before forwarding G/FO personnel action packages for Presidential, Secretary of Defense, or USD(P&R) approval or Senate confirmation.[44] The NCIC, which is maintained by the FBI, serves as an electronic clearinghouse of crime data. Criminal justice agencies enter the information into the NCIC so that law enforcement agencies can use it for law enforcement purposes. It is not a criminal history record database; rather, the database captures the nation's current "hot files" (i.e., files related to current law enforcement issues). The database is made up of 21 files, including seven property files (e.g., records of stolen property, such as guns and license plates) and 14 persons files (e.g., the National Sex Offender Registry and files on missing persons, known and suspected terrorists, protection orders, and identity theft).[45] Authorized users can search for information about individuals by entering their names and dates of birth.

Strengths, Limitations, and Issues
The FBI has not allowed the Services to use the NCIC to search for adverse and reportable information for military officer personnel actions. To learn why, we spoke with two experts on the FBI databases, including the FBI compact officer, whose job is to insist and ensure that federal agencies are complying with the law and policy governing the use of the databases. A

---

[44] DoDI 1320.04, 2014, Enclosure 5, p. 19.

[45] FBI, "National Crime Information Center (NCIC)," webpage, undated a.

search of the NCIC for noncriminal justice purposes is not authorized. Any agency that has access to the NCIC must be audited every two years, and the experts each speculated that it was likely that the Services were informed during audits that name and date-of-birth searches of the NCIC for personnel actions, such as promotions, are not permitted.

The FBI has two other relevant databases.[46] The FBI Interstate Identification Index is a criminal history record database; however, a name and date-of-birth search can be done only by criminal justice agencies and only for criminal justice purposes. We were advised that the FBI is not likely to view promotion or assignment as a criminal justice purpose.

The FBI's Next Generation Identification (NGI) System also contains criminal history record information.[47] Authorized agencies could search the NGI System for noncriminal justice purposes, such as for licensing, employment, and regulatory reasons;[48] however, these agencies would need to submit fingerprints as a basis for returning the results. The NGI System is searchable only by fingerprint (rather than by name and date of birth) to ensure that the match is to the right person. Of further importance, to be able to use the NGI System, DoD would have to have the authority to submit fingerprints for that purpose. State agencies must have a specific state statute in line with Public Law 92-544. That law gives governmental agencies within states the authority to send fingerprints to the FBI and the FBI authority to respond back with a criminal history, if there is one. OSD and the Services could potentially search the NGI System to inform their officer personnel actions, but there must be a federal statute that permits this.[49]

As a source of criminal history records, the NGI System might be more relevant than the NCIC for identifying adverse and reportable information. However, it is possible that the new, ongoing security clearance review processes would meet DoD and SASC requirements. Regardless of whether DoD or the SASC chooses to replace the NCIC requirement with the NGI System, the next version of DoDI 1320.04 will need to omit the requirement to check the NCIC database files.

Central Clearance Facility Records

Types and Sources of Adverse and Reportable Information
Security clearances are granted after "a determination that an individual . . . is eligible for access to classified national security information."[50] The guiding policies for the Central Clearance Facility are DoD Manual 5200.02, *Procedures for the DoD Personnel Security Program (PSP)*, and DoDD 5220.6, *Defense Industrial Personnel Security Clearance Review Program*.[51]

---

[46] One additional FBI database is checked for the transfer of firearms by federally licensed dealers and therefore is not relevant in this context.

[47] FBI, "Next Generation Identification (NGI)," webpage, undated b.

[48] Ernest J. Babcock, *Next Generation Identification (NGI)—Retention and Searching of Noncriminal Justice Fingerprint Submissions*, Washington, D.C.: Federal Bureau of Investigation, February 20, 2015.

[49] The National Crime Prevention and Privacy Compact Act covers authorized uses; see 34 U.S.C. 40311–40316.

[50] Michelle D. Christensen, *Security Clearance Process: Answers to Frequently Asked Questions*, Washington, D.C.: U.S. Government Accountability Office, R43216, October 7, 2016, p. 1.

[51] DoD Manual 5200.02, *Procedures for the DoD Personnel Security Program (PSP)*, Washington: D.C.: U.S. Department of Defense, April 3, 2017; and DoDD 5220.6, *Defense Industrial Personnel Security Clearance Review Program*, Washing-

The DoD clearance process requires the applicant to complete an online Standard Form (SF) 86, the "Questionnaire for National Security Positions." The questionnaire gathers self-reported biographical information, including a ten-year residence history, an education and employment history, a criminal history, foreign contact and activities, personal references, family members, psychological and emotional health, drug and alcohol use, and a financial record.[52] The information is provided to the Defense Counterintelligence and Security Agency within DoD,[53] and an investigation is initiated. The background investigation includes verification of submitted information, National Agency Checks (including FBI), searches of public records, and interviews. The information from the background investigation is provided to the DoD Consolidated Adjudication Facility (CAF), which determines whether the individual can be granted a security clearance.

Given the nature of the information investigated for a clearance, it is possible that an individual's security clearance review could yield information that meets the DoDI 1320.04 policy definition of adverse or reportable information. In some cases, the information might not rise to the level of a crime but might still affect the individual's clearance status. For example, excessive alcohol consumption or failure to live within one's financial means could present national security concerns but, in and of themselves, are not crimes. Although the DoD CAF's main concern is whether an individual's "continued [clearance] eligibility is clearly consistent with the interests of national security,"[54] the CAF is also responsible for reporting any derogatory information to counterintelligence or law enforcement authorities as appropriate.[55] Moreover, derogatory information is "referred to the commander or the security professional of the DoD organization to which the person is assigned for duty."[56]

If an adjudication facility suspends an individual's clearance eligibility, the facility must notify the individual affected in writing and provide a brief statement of the reasons for suspension of eligibility. The individual must then sign a receipt acknowledging the suspension notification.[57] Individuals also will be provided with the opportunity to appeal the determination.

Strengths, Limitations, and Issues

Central Clearance Facility records overlap with and complement other sources of information within DoD. In particular, the background investigations tap into civilian sources of information, such as law enforcement databases; financial records; and thorough interviews with friends, neighbors, and employers (particularly relevant for reserve officers). Also, security clearance holders are required to self-report incidents that might affect their clearances, such as arrests, lawsuits, financial problems, or mandated substance abuse or psychological counsel-

---

ton, D.C.: U.S. Department of Defense, January 2, 1992, Administrative Reissuance Incorporating Through Change 4, April 20, 1999.

[52] Information about the form is publicly available at U.S. Office of Personnel Management, *Completing Your Investigation Request in e-QIP: Guide for the Standard Form (SF) 86*, Washington, D.C., July 2018.

[53] Formerly, this information was reported to the National Background Investigations Bureau within the Office of Personnel Management.

[54] DoD Manual 5200.02, 2017, p. 57.

[55] DoD Manual 5200.02, 2017, p. 57.

[56] DoD Manual 5200.02, 2017, p. 56.

[57] DoD Manual 5200.02, 2017, p. 58.

ing as a result of problematic work or other behavior.[58] Recent changes suggest that this security review process is likely to become an even more valuable source of adverse and reportable information.

The management of the security clearance review process has changed significantly since the 2010 RAND review and the publication of DoDI 1320.04 in 2014. Prior to 2013, each of the Services managed a CAF processing individuals' access to classified information.[59] As the result of a Base Realignment and Closure decision in 2012, all of the Services' non-intelligence CAFs were consolidated within the newly structured DoD CAF. The DoD CAF processes the paperwork and investigations necessary to administer and maintain security clearances. In October 2019, the DoD CAF was transferred from the Office of Personnel Management to the Defense Counterintelligence and Security Agency.[60] Before and after that transition, major ongoing efforts have targeted a backlog of investigations and the average clearance review timeline.

Security clearance processes are currently evolving through the "Trusted Workforce 2.0" framework developed by the Suitability and Security Clearance Performance Accountability Council. Whereas personnel were previously subject to periodic reinvestigations at five- and ten-year intervals, depending on the type of clearance, the new process is expected to enable continuous vetting (and, where possible, automated checks) for determinations of security status.[61] The implication for adverse and reportable information is that, with ongoing security reviews, adverse or reportable information may be revealed in a much timelier manner. This could eliminate a potential gap in coverage caused by periodic reinvestigation intervals not always aligning with the promotion process.[62] These changes might have implications for the personnel processes outlined in DoDI 1320.04, in terms of keeping the data checks current. Additionally, if for military officers the continuous vetting process will frequently check the FBI's NGI System or receive automatic alerts to any fingerprint matches, then a requirement for the Services to conduct a separate FBI NGI System database search would be redundant and unnecessary.

One issue raised by DoD representatives is that the retirement procedures described in DoDI 1320.04 do not indicate any process for how or whether retiring G/FOs with adverse or reportable information should be evaluated to potentially have their security clearances revoked upon retirement, or which parties would be responsible for doing so. Policy permits retiring G/FOs to retain a security clearance for up to one year to access classified information regarding a specific DoD program or mission.[63] But the retirement personnel action processes or postretirement investigations might uncover misconduct or other reasons that certain officers should not be permitted to continue to advise or work with DoD.

---

[58] Defense Counterintelligence and Security Agency, "Self-Report a Security Change or Concern," webpage, undated b.

[59] Defense Counterintelligence and Security Agency, "History," webpage, undated a.

[60] Defense Counterintelligence and Security Agency, undated a.

[61] Aaron Boyd, "The Security Clearance Process Is About to Get Its Biggest Overhaul in 50 Years," Nextgov, February 28, 2019.

[62] We did not meet with representatives in a classified setting to discuss continuous vetting and its potential to eliminate the information gap.

[63] DoD Manual 5200.02, 2017, p. 22.

Judge Advocate and General Counsel Records

Types and Sources of Adverse and Reportable Information

JAs and GCs are attorneys within OSD and the Services. JAs are military officers who focus on military personnel legal issues and matters concerning military missions. Their specializations include military justice, administrative law, legal assistance, and claims. Across the Services, JAs provide legal advice (privileged communication) to their respective commands and to service members. The GC for each military department serves as the chief legal adviser to the secretary and other senior leaders. GCs with each Office of the General Counsel are federal civilian employees, and their legal specializations span such areas as government contracts, international transactions, labor relations, fiscal law, and arms control. The military departments' GCs are responsible for their respective ethics and integrity programs and alternate dispute resolution programs.

Strengths, Limitations, and Issues

The Service JA and GC representatives with whom we met provide legal and regulatory reviews of the contents of the personnel action packages, which include information from the other data sources listed in this chapter. They also help ensure completeness of the files. These attorneys do not conduct their own investigations or seek to verify the information contained in the packages. The legal reviews can be time-consuming, especially when the investigative materials are lengthy. From start to finish, a dozen or more attorneys might scrutinize a G/FO's personnel package. Multiple reviews are a strength when different attorneys apply different types of expertise or leadership priorities to their reviews, and they increase the likelihood that mistakes or omissions are caught before the package is submitted to DoD. Multiple reviews could be a limitation, however, if the legal reviews become overly redundant and extend the review timelines considerably in cases in which fewer attorneys could have achieved essentially the same outcome. We did not independently assess or delve into this issue, but we note that several offices raised the question of whether a more efficient and effective legal review process is possible.

Records of Command-Directed Investigations and Their Outcomes

Types and Sources of Adverse and Reportable Information

Leaders in each of the Services use an array of administrative tools to counsel or discipline personnel, including command investigations, informal counseling statements, memoranda of reprimand (different types for increasing levels of severity), personnel evaluations, and nonjudicial punishment under Article 15 of the Uniform Code of Military Justice (UCMJ).[64] The less formal forms of administrative action—those taken by commanders below the rank of O-5, often affecting more-junior personnel and involving minor misconduct or performance issues—typically result in documentation that is kept in local files. Unless the behavior is repeated or escalated or other problems emerge, the document may not enter a service member's official military personnel file, follow the service member to the next assignment, or be

---

[64] An Article 15 is a form of nonjudicial punishment available to commanders to resolve allegations of minor misconduct without escalating the misconduct to a higher form of discipline, such as a court martial (10 U.S.C. 815).

discoverable by the Services when they perform their checks for adverse or reportable information. Substantiated command investigations of personnel at or above the grade of O-4, memoranda of reprimand from G/FOs, and nonjudicial punishment are generally expected to be recorded in an official database and are therefore discoverable through Service searches for adverse information. More-formal types of administrative action may also be annotated or reflected on a service member's personnel evaluation, which is part of the personnel file and part of the record considered by promotion boards.

Under the UCMJ, commanders have the inherent authority to investigate matters under their command to maintain good order and discipline.[65] CDIs are not appropriate in cases in which a commander believes that a service member's conduct is criminal; in those cases, a law enforcement agency should investigate the incident. Although the UCMJ applies to all of the Services, each Service maintains different policies and procedures for executing CDIs. The differences between CDI approaches are captured in Table 5.1.

Air Force Instruction (AFI) 90-301 grants the authority to initiate a CDI to a commander at the squadron level and above. The command appoints an investigating officer, supported by a legal adviser. The investigating officer interviews witnesses and prepares findings for the commander. The commander then provides a memo indicating concurrence or nonconcurrence.[66] As noted earlier, since 2018 the Air Force has required that all commanders notify their IGs when they are initiating a CDI or another inquiry involving an officer. The IGs will track the status and the outcomes of the CDIs, and the Air Force headquarters-level IGs have central access to the IG data from across the Service.

Table 5.1
Service Differences in Centralized Command-Directed Investigation Information Accessible by Service Headquarters for Adverse and Reportable Information Checks

Service	Available Information	Centralized Location	Who Enters the Information
Air Force	All CDIs of officers as soon as they are opened	IG database	Local IG
Marine Corps	All CDIs of officers as soon as they are opened	Officer Disciplinary Notebook	Local SJA
Army	Completed, commander-approved, substantiated adverse findings for O-4 to O-6 officers and for high-profile cases	Adverse Information Pilot Program database	Local SJA
Navy	No central source of command administrative (JAGMAN) investigations of officers	None	Not applicable

SOURCE: Author meetings with Service representatives, 2019.
NOTES: SJA = staff judge advocate. *JAGMAN* refers to the Navy's JAG Instruction (JAGINST) 5800.7F, *Manual of the Judge Advocate General*, Washington, D.C.: Department of the Navy, June 26, 2012. Also, since this study was conducted (2019), the Adverse Information Pilot Program has become the Army Adverse Information Program.

---

[65] DoD, *Manual for Courts-Martial United States (2019 Edition)*, Washington, D.C., 2019, p. I-1.

[66] AFI 90-301, 2018; and Balaji L. Narain and Dustin Banks, "Administrative Investigations and Non-Judicial Punishment in Joint Environments," *The Reporter*, May 23, 2019.

Within the Army, a CDI (or *AR 15-6*) is recorded in a centrally accessible database only for O-4 to O-6 officers once the investigation has been completed and commander-approved and once the findings have been substantiated,[67] making this information adverse under the current DoDI 1320.04 definition. Policy states that the servicing SJA or legal adviser will provide a summary of the finding and the filing location to the Office of the Judge Advocate General. The policy also provides instructions on filing requirements for high-profile cases because "[r]eports of proceedings in serious, complex, or high-profile cases that result in national media interest, Congressional investigation, and/or substantive changes in Army policies or procedures have value for historical and lessons-learned purposes."[68]

AR 27-10 outlines the policy guidance for nonjudicial punishment (NJP). AR 27-10 states, "Use of nonjudicial punishment is proper in all cases involving minor offenses in which nonpunitive measures are considered inadequate or inappropriate."[69] NJP in the Army can take one of two forms: summarized proceedings or formal proceedings; formal proceedings are more serious.[70] In the case of summarized findings, the proceedings are summarized on Department of the Army (DA) Form 2627-1 and are maintained locally in an NJP file. The summary is then destroyed at the end of two years from the date of the punishment or upon the officer's transfer from the unit, whichever comes first.[71] In a formal proceeding, the accused individual is subject to an Article 15 hearing, after which the commander submits a DA Form 2627, "Record of Proceedings Under Article 15, UCMJ," to the officer's Official Military Personnel File.[72]

Navy and Marine Corps personnel are subject to the Department of the Navy's JAGINST 5800.7F, *Manual of the Judge Advocate General*, commonly referred to as the JAGMAN. If NJP is administered as a result of a CDI, the JAGMAN articulates that "appropriate service-record entries should be made and signed by appropriate personnel."[73] If upon investigation it is determined that the accused conducted wrongdoing, a commander can file a censure (punitive or nonpunitive) in writing. The written admonition or reprimand is then filed as part of the officer's official service record.[74]

Although the Navy and the Marine Corps are subject to the JAGMAN, records of NJP are processed differently within the two Services. Within the U.S. Navy, NJP records are reported to Navy Personnel Command (PERS-4834) if the officer is in the grade of O-6 or above, if the officer is in the grade of O-5 with special court-martial convening authority, or if, in the judgment of the superior commander, the incident could generate significant adverse publicity or the findings will result in formal disciplinary action.[75] But there is no central database of Navy JAGMAN investigation records that tracks these records across the Service.

[67] AR 15-6, *Procedures for Administrative Investigations and Boards of Officers*, Washington, D.C.: Department of the Army, April 1, 2016, p. 29.

[68] AR 15-6, 2016, p. 29.

[69] AR 27-10, *Military Justice*, Washington, D.C.: Department of the Army, June 24, 1996, p. 7.

[70] AR 27-10, 1996, pp. 10–11.

[71] AR 27-10, 1996, p. 10.

[72] AR 27-10, 1996, p. 23.

[73] JAGINST 5800.7F, 2012, p. 1–18.

[74] JAGINST 5800.7F, 2012, p. 1–23.

[75] JAGINST 5800.7F, 2012, p. 1–33.

In the case of the Marine Corps, all Marine officer misconduct must be reported by an SJA to the Headquarters, Marine Corps, Judge Advocate Division, Military Personnel Law Branch (JPL) under Marine Corps Order (MCO) 5800.16.[76] The MCO requires use of the Commandant of the Marine Corps's Officer Disciplinary Notebook (ODN), a database used to "track officer misconduct and substandard performance."[77] Initial reports must be made at the time credible information is presented, but ODN entries are not included in the Official Military Personnel File until and unless they are substantiated. The ODN captures the details and tracks the progress of an allegation. Files are updated by the 20th of each month to reflect the status and the findings, regardless of whether an accusation is substantiated.[78] Therefore, the Marine Corps maintains a historical record that allows it to identify when and how any adverse or reportable information was handled at any point in the process.

Strengths, Limitations, and Issues

CDIs and subsequent leadership actions are important in that they provide leaders with an opportunity to correct problems in their units and counsel and develop their service members. Moreover, not every mistake or minor incident or infraction warrants a record in an officer's performance evaluation; mistakes and misjudgments are inevitable over the course of a career, and officers can learn and grow from their mistakes.

CDIs present challenges with respect to consistent application. When more-junior officers are put in the position of investigating senior officers—even officers above them in the chain of command—it can generate a conflict of interest. Also, in cases of substantiated allegations, commanders have the *option* to discipline their subordinate and thus may choose not to do so. Concerns about harming the subordinate's career can factor into that decision. Additionally, CDI approaches vary across the Services. These differences can disadvantage officers in Services with more-stringent record-keeping systems that track these CDIs and their outcomes.

Potential Adverse and Reportable Information Gaps

DoDI 1320.04 policy revisions aim to close gaps in reporting practices for adverse and reportable information to ensure compliance with statutory intent and instill confidence in the reliability of information reported in officer personnel action packages. In studying the reporting policies and processes, we asked about the types of data sources that are checked and learned that certain sources of information are not normally searched or are not required to be searched and reported. However, these sources could contain information that might surface later. Thus, we briefly document those sources in this section for consideration. We are mindful that the current data check requirements are already challenging for some organizations to meet in a timely manner and that there will always be more places one could look. This section describes only those sources we asked about during our research.

---

[76] MCO 5800.16-V15, *Legal Support and Administration Manual*, Washington, D.C.: Marine Corps, August 8, 2018.

[77] MCO 5800.16-V15, 2018, p. 1–11.

[78] MCO 5800.16-V15, 2018, p. 1–13.

Information from Other Services

Our review of current Service and DoD processes for identifying and reporting adverse and reportable information highlighted potential blind spots stemming from multi-Service activities and Service-segregated data systems. Service members work not only in settings led by their own Service or a joint command but also in multi-Service settings. This can happen, for example, when officers are deployed; assigned to the Pentagon or an installation belonging to another Service; or in multi-Service training exercises, temporary duty assignments, and professional military education.

None of the Services systematically check the records of the other Services for adverse and reportable information reporting requirements. Barriers to directly checking the records would include segregated databases, unfamiliar software, and information access controls for data safeguarding and security (if not also cultural norms). Because all complaints against senior officials are supposed to be reported to the DoD OIG, this issue is less relevant for officers already in pay grades O-7 and above. This issue speaks more to the completeness of the record checks for the years prior to promotion to O-7 (recall that adverse information spans the previous ten years for information not previously reported to the Senate) and for requirements to furnish selection boards with adverse information.

U.S. Department of Defense and Service Civilian Employment Records of Reserve Component Personnel

Most reserve-component officers are part-time military personnel, though some do serve full-time in Active Guard Reserve positions.[79] National Guard and reserve officers may have other forms of employment. Dual-status technicians also hold a federal civilian position that requires as condition of employment that they maintain membership in the Selected Reserve.[80] Other reserve-component personnel work as civilian employees for a Service, DoD, or another agency as civilians not under the military technician status. Still other reserve-component personnel work for other government organizations or public or private companies or are self-employed.

The differences in duty status and employment result in varying levels of access to potential adverse and reportable information for reserve-component officers. Because officers serving full-time in the military in Active Guard Reserve positions are governed by the UCMJ at all times, the Services have greater access to adverse and reportable information regarding those officers than officers in other duty statuses. Military personnel records are kept in separate files from civilian employment records. There are no integrated files for individuals that contain both their military and civilian employment activities. Selection boards review only the military record, not any civilian employment records. Across our interviews, we asked whether adverse and reportable information searches for personnel actions include checking Service or DoD civilian employment records of any officers who are also Service or DoD civilian employees. No representatives were aware of any such searches. We were told that sometimes misconduct or complaints against officers serving in their civilian capacity will come to the attention of their military chain of command and perhaps be reflected in their military records. This might occur, for example, when the individual's civilian position and guard or

---

[79] It is worth noting that since the terrorist attacks of September 11, 2001, reservists have been increasingly mobilized at unprecedented levels. For more information, see Theodore F. Figinski, "The Effect of Potential Activations on the Employment of Military Reservists: Evidence from a Field Experiment," *ILR Review*, Vol. 70, No. 4, August 2017, pp. 1037–1056.

[80] 10 U.S.C. 10216.

reserve position are in the same unit or location. This could prompt an investigation of such behavior on the military side as well, or a substantiated allegation could have implications for military service (e.g., the person's security clearance), but not necessarily. Although it would certainly be impractical to contact the countless other employers of part-time National Guard and reserve officers, with sufficient resources it might be practical and worthwhile to search the civilian employee records already in Service or DoD possession.

Professional License Investigations

Professional license investigations of officers in applicable career fields could be another source of adverse or reportable information not explicitly required by policy. Our meetings with DoD and Service representatives involved in the military officer personnel action processes indicate that the respective offices do not check for such investigations when preparing personnel packages for military officer actions covered by DoDI 1320.04. The exception, however, is that JAG offices already involved in reviewing personnel packages do have visibility on their organization's own professional misconduct investigations of military lawyers.

For example, many health care professions—including physicians, nurses, surgeons, pharmacists, physician assistants, and mental health care providers—require professional licenses. Officers in such professions could be under investigation for possible professional misconduct, impairment, or lack of professional competence, and possible outcomes could include limitation on their scope of practice, loss of privileges to provide care at a certain facility, loss of credentials, or financial loss to the government through malpractice claims or death and disability payments.[81] According to policy, such investigations should be entered and tracked in a central Defense Health Agency electronic database, the Centralized Credentials Quality Assurance System.[82]

For guard and reserve officers holding professional credentials, there could be civilian investigations and disciplinary actions related to these officers' civilian professional activities about which military organizations are not aware at the time of the proposed military personnel action.

It was beyond the scope of our study to catalog the officer career fields for which this question might apply or investigate databases that might contain professional license investigation information. We share in this section the examples we asked Service representatives about as we sought to learn whether these investigations were being captured by any of the Service or DoD offices involved in the adverse and reportable information checks.

Civilian Criminal or Civil Legal Filings or Investigative Records

Ideally, the military department secretaries would be aware of any unfavorable civilian legal activity or allegations of misconduct before providing an exemplary conduct certification and recommending a personnel action for a given officer. However, civilian criminal or civil legal filings might not come to the military's attention at the time they occur. Examples provided to us included arrests for driving under the influence or for disorderly conduct while on leave. Publicly accessible documents associated with divorce, child custody battles, or civil lawsuits could include alleged or substantiated misconduct not brought to the attention of the Service

[81] DoD Manual 6025.13, *Medical Quality Assurance (MQA) and Clinical Quality Management in the Military Health Care System (MHS)*, Washington, D.C.: U.S. Department of Defense, October 29, 2013.

[82] DoD Manual 6025.13, 2013, Enclosure 5.

or DoD. Such information could be revealed later in the personnel process, which could be problematic for the nomination if it first arises once the package is already at the White House or the Senate.

There are a few ways in which the current system can identify this information. One possibility is through the self-reporting requirement. The FY 2006 NDAA introduced a requirement that military officers and senior enlisted personnel (E-7 to E-9) self-report a conviction by U.S. law enforcement for any violation of U.S. criminal law, regardless of whether they were on duty at the time of the incident, and that the new regulations should apply uniformly across the armed forces.[83] At the time the FY 2006 was enacted, each of the Services followed this requirement. However, in 2010, the U.S. Navy encountered challenges to the legality of a policy mandating self-reporting of arrests and convictions, given service members' constitutional right not to self-incriminate.[84] Through a Chief of Naval Operations Instruction, the U.S. Navy (the Service) revised its policy, and this revised version was upheld in subsequent court challenges because of the added safeguards protecting the self-reporter from further questioning and from military prosecution as a result of self-reporting.[85] The Marine Corps has not updated its policy, and legal analysis from 2018 suggests that other Service policies also might be open to challenges.[86] Furthermore, the analysis notes that the Army and Air Force policies require reporting of convictions but not arrests. The point is that these self-reporting requirements are limited, might not be followed (particularly by individuals who do not demonstrate exemplary conduct), might not be consistent across the Services, and might be challenged in the future.

As noted earlier, however, individuals with a security clearance are required to self-report information potentially relevant for their clearance, such as arrests or lawsuits. Additionally, the new continuous vetting security review process (in contrast to past periodic reinvestigations) offers the promise that such information could surface independently of self-reports.

Another way civilian criminal or civil legal filings or investigative records could surface is in response to nomination lists publicly released by the Service or DoD or published on the SASC website, although these lists are published after the military department secretary has already approved the officers.[87] Because of growing concerns about the complaint system serving as a tool for those with malicious intent (which we discuss later), the offices we met with noted that the Services have become wary of sharing this information early in the process.[88] Deferring public announcements to once the President has approved the nomination or when the nomination is posted on the SASC website has the benefit of limiting the window in which malicious actors can target individual officers; however, the limited window also means that legitimate unfavorable information might appear after the package has left DoD, when a con-

---

[83]   Pub. L. 109-163, 2006, Sec. 554.

[84]   *United States v. Serianne*, 69 M.J. 8, 9.

[85]   Carman A. Leone, "Ordered to Self-Incriminate: The Unconstitutionality of Self-Report Policies in the Armed Forces," *Air Force Law Review*, Vol. 78, 2018, pp. 125–167.

[86]   Leone, 2018.

[87]   U.S. Senate Committee on Armed Services, "Nominations," webpage, undated b.

[88]   For example, see Ben Werner, "Navy Stopped Publicly Announcing Flag Officer Nominations, Citing Policy Review," *USNI News*, last updated February 28, 2019.

stituent contacts a member of Congress with information. Studying these options, their risks, and possible mitigation strategies and courses of action was beyond our scope for this study.

Finally, the Services and DoD must balance available resources and staffing with the variety of potential sources of adverse or reportable information. It would not be practical for the Services or DoD to attempt to identify every legal document across the United States and abroad that might be associated with a senior military officer to review the content of each file for any potentially undiscovered adverse or reportable information.

The Internet

As defined in DoDI 1320.04, *reportable information* includes "credible information . . . [of the officer's] involvement or affiliation with a significant event that is widely known to the general public or members of Congress that brings discredit upon or calls into question the integrity of members of the DoD."[89] Although some events are so widely covered in the news that they are seemingly ubiquitous, a particular officer's connection with an event might not be widely known. Additionally, some events, such as an incident that received wide news coverage within a state or in a professional community but was not publicized more broadly, are widely known only in certain contexts or groups. We found that no Service or DoD office was required to conduct internet searches to identify widely known events, and almost none did so. A nominee's affiliation with such an event could be discovered by the SASC or presented to a senator during the confirmation process and thus lead to Senate questions about why the Services and DoD did not report that information. We explored why internet searches are not a part of the process to check for potential adverse or reportable information. Several explanations were offered:

- The policy does not require it.
- It would be unfair to individual officers if not all Services were searching the internet.
- There is uncertainty regarding the legality of such searches for these purposes.
- It is unclear what the appropriate search procedures would be.
- Other data checks and legal reviews are already labor-intensive and consume the timeline given the workload and personnel assigned.
- Widely known information usually comes to the offices' attention in other ways: It is reported through an official channel, colleagues forward news items to the office for its awareness, or office staff members read about the information in the course of following current events and DoD-related news.

DoD might want to consider the use of internet checks within the process of identifying adverse and reportable information, but the requirement would not be a simple matter. If DoD determines that internet searches are appropriate, the Services will need specific guidance to standardize the process and meet expectations. First, the Services will need to know which tools, search engines, or websites are appropriate and necessary for executing such searches. Second, the Services will need guidance on how to implement a sufficient search for adverse and reportable information (e.g., how many pages of Google search results they should review). Third, the Services will need guidance on how or whether to gauge the credibility of sources, because the most-popular search results could include blogs or social media posts in addition

---

[89] DoDI 1320.04, 2014, p. 17.

to stories from reputable long-standing news sources. Also, even established, reputable news sources can print factual errors, so there is the question of whether independent verification of the information would be required or allowed.

Even with such guidance, there could be additional limitations. Staff searching on government computers might not locate certain mentions visible to the public, because the system blocks inappropriate content (such as pornographic websites) and less secure websites (such as those without current security certificates). Also, internet searches are in part tailored to users based on previous web activity, so results will not necessarily be identical across individuals or devices. Thus, individuals could be faulted for omitting "front-page" stories that did not appear on their own front pages of search engine results.

The process of examining the internet for adverse or reportable information could be time-intensive, particularly if those performing the searches are to confirm that the officer in question is the person being mentioned in the search result. Searches for offensive or inappropriate images or images capturing misconduct will be much more challenging than the text-based searches that are the foundation of search engines. Lastly, there are many social media platforms that could be checked (such as Facebook, Twitter, and Instagram) and that evolve over time and in popularity.

Professional online reputation management companies may have developed methods for conducting such searches that address some of the challenges that we have outlined, but a more in-depth exploration of this topic was outside the scope of our study.

The bottom line is that there are reasons to conduct an internet search for officer reportable information; however, any discussion of including this requirement in the DoD policy should consider the potential complexities of the task.

Personal Emails and Texts Through Military and Nonmilitary Devices

In some highly publicized cases, the evidence of officer misconduct that comes to light is documented in emails and texts. These sources can reveal, for example, inappropriate relationships, such as adultery and fraternization, that violate military law (Article 134 of the UCMJ), which defines them as prejudicial to good order and discipline and conduct bringing discredit upon the armed forces. Email and text exchanges may be searched in the context of investigations; however, such a search is not conducted as a part of any routine data checks for any of these officer personnel actions. Given the frequency with which email and texts are used for communication today, and given that it would require more than just a word search to assess the nature of the content, such an undertaking would be tremendously labor-intensive, expensive, and impractical.

Concerns About "Weaponizing" Complaints

Representatives from the various offices across the Services and DoD with whom we met raised concerns that complaints were becoming a means to intentionally disrupt officers' careers—what is referred to as *weaponizing* the complaint system. We note that we did not actively seek to learn about this research topic; rather, it was raised spontaneously by most offices with whom we spoke. There was a sense among those involved in these personnel processes of growing awareness across the force, and particularly among officers, that open allegations can stop or delay confirmations. Especially once an officer's nomination has been made public by the Senate, spikes of new complaints can derail the final stage of the confirmation process.

Complaints that are anonymous can make it difficult to identify weaponized complaints from the same individual making multiple complaints against an officer or submitting a complaint that they know has already been formally adjudicated through an official process.[90] Anonymous complaints can also make investigations difficult because there is not an identified complainant to contact. Such complaints also affect demands on Service and DoD personnel processing officer personnel action packages and increase the caseload of investigative agencies, such as the IG and EEO offices.

We did not independently study the presence of weaponized complaints, and we do not have firsthand accounts, studies, or other evidence of individuals' motives for filing complaints. However, the pervasiveness of these beliefs and corresponding strong concerns indicate an important topic for further study. It is also worth considering ways to address such concerns, such as additional resource allocation to expedite new investigations for individuals in the confirmation process.

Summary

Types and Sources of Adverse and Reportable Information

The military department secretaries must certify that the officers they recommend for positive personnel actions have demonstrated exemplary conduct. For actions for G/FOs (and promotion to O-7), DoD policy requires that secretaries certify that DoD, Service, and state IG; EEO; EO; NCIC; Central Clearance Facility; JAG and GC; and other Service investigative files have been reviewed. These records hold evidence of various types of violations of rules, regulations, and laws, including both substantiated and unsubstantiated allegations. They also include complaints about leaders that are actually just dissatisfaction with their decisions that are within their purview, such as selecting one individual over another for a special assignment, rather than actual violations of any policy or law.

There is some overlap in the types of information covered by each source, and there is coordination across some of the listed organizations. A matter might be raised with one organization but referred or delegated to another. For example, the DoD OIG might defer action on a complaint if the complainant has submitted the same complaint to another agency with relevant processes, such as a Service or DoD EEO entity for EEO-related issues, and the IG will track the result. In another example, all organizations must forward complaints against senior officials to the DoD OIG. Unless the officer is at the O-9 or O-10 level, the DoD OIG could permit a Service IG to conduct the investigation and oversee that work. JAs and GCs review and advise the commanders and IGs on legal aspects of the investigations. The Central Clearance Facility security review information includes checks of FBI records on activities involving civilian law enforcement or criminal investigations.

---

[90] Anonymous options can be important for encouraging reporting among those with legitimate complaints who would otherwise be afraid of reprisal or other negative consequences for coming forward. We do not intend to imply that anonymous complaints should not be permitted.

Overall Strengths, Limitations, and Issues

The updated policy (DoDI 1320.04) is specific about which data sources must be checked for possible adverse and reportable information. It is a strength that many data systems, which cover a variety of types of misconduct, reporting channels, and authorities, are checked. Some sources overlap in the types of information they contain. That the IG investigation must be periodically refreshed can help catch issues emerging during the personnel action review process.

There is no single data set containing all of the DoD and Service personnel data that must be checked. Available sources of data pertinent to adverse and reportable information exist in disparate locations within DoD, the Services, and other sources. The current DoDI 1320.04 requirement to include FBI NCIC checks presents a challenge to the Services because the database is not authorized for use for employment purposes and does not provide criminal history data. Updates to the clearance review process, moving from a periodic reinvestigation to an ongoing vetting process, might help the Services fill that gap.

Many Service data systems are inefficient and thus labor-intensive. Database limitations require staff to manually input individual names rather than providing a mechanism through which to upload multiple names simultaneously. Section 503 of the FY 2020 NDAA, which requires the Services to expand the furnishing of adverse information to additional promotion selection boards (promotion to O-4 and above for active-component officers and to O-6 and above for reserve-component officers rather than just to boards considering promotion to G/FO ranks),[91] will greatly increase the labor required to perform manual searches for adverse information.

The EEO data systems were designed to track cases by the complainant, and they require that a name is entered precisely the way the name is recorded in the system (including or not including a middle name, middle initial, or suffix) to render a matching result. It is possible for adverse or reportable information to be overlooked if an officer's name is not entered in the same way that it is recorded. A further problem is that the complainant might refer to the accused by position or title rather than by name (e.g., "my wing commander"), thus making it difficult to identify potential adverse or reportable information using name searches. The risk to the Services is the possibility that Service Chiefs or secretaries of the military departments might certify to the SASC that an officer does not have an open case, when in fact the Service was just unable to identify it because of search constraints. Furthermore, investigations can take months to complete, and complaint processes can even take years to move through all of the necessary steps, particularly when early attempts at resolution have been unsuccessful.

Some allegations clearly are not credible and can be resolved relatively quickly, such as cases of mistaken identity for individuals with similar names. EEO accusations can take years to resolve, however, and can result in settlements and EEOC final decisions that do not even state whether a particular officer was responsible for the discrimination. In most cases, the EEOC judge does not conclude that there was discrimination.

CDIs are not explicitly included in the required data checks, although they could fall under the category of other Service investigative files. These investigations are tools to help the commanders understand what is happening in their units, and the investigations are conducted by officers who might be trained to the task but typically are not professional investiga-

---

[91] Public Law 116-92, 2019.

tors. Commanders, who are more senior and more experienced than their CDI investigators, might legitimately disagree with the conclusions the investigating officer drew. Commanders might take actions to guide and mentor their subordinates, never intending for those actions to later have ramifications. CDI information is unevenly accessible by the different Service headquarters. The expectation across the Services is that, for serious behaviors, the commander will ensure that the misconduct is included in the officer's record in some form and is reflected in the officer's performance evaluation.

Lastly, some information gaps will always exist. DoD will need to consider whether any additional data sources, such as professional license investigations, Service or DoD civilian employee records, or the internet, would be worth the resources and time to systematically address.

CHAPTER SIX

Senate Armed Services Committee Processes and Perspectives

As described in Chapter One, congressional authorities and responsibilities regarding military officer appointments and promotions are laid forth in both statute and law, with a basis in the U.S. Constitution. Congressional requirements are further codified on an annual basis through the passage of the NDAA,[1] and requirements can be transmitted more informally to OSD and the Services. The SASC is central to the Senate's role in ensuring compliance with the law and providing oversight of DoD, the Department of the Army, the Department of the Navy (which includes the Marine Corps), and the Department of the Air Force (which now includes the Space Force).[2] Commissioned officers are nominated by the President, and the Senate confirms nominations for all active-component officers to the pay grades of O-4 and above and all reserve officers to the pay grades of O-6 and above. The Senate further confirms Federal Recognition for National Guard officers for the pay grades of O-6 and above. The SASC is the committee that reviews and considers the officer nomination packages submitted for Senate confirmation. By the time the Senate receives a personnel action package, the nomination has already been approved by the Service, DoD, and the President. Although SASC policies and processes are not the focus of our report, for greater context this chapter provides a broad overview of how personnel packages are managed once they arrive at the SASC, with attention to how adverse and reportable information files are managed and used.

This chapter also notes further opportunities for DoD and Service policies, processes, and practices to better align with Senate adverse and reportable information reporting expectations. The Services and DoD will never review officer files with the exact same lens as the SASC. The goal of DoD policy is to help ensure that the various offices involved in preparing personnel action packages for Senate confirmation provide information that meets expectations as best they can and are responsive to SASC requests for additional information. Ultimately, close alignment in approach or understanding matters, because when DoD does not send all of the types of information that SASC members expect to receive or does not send that information in a timely manner, the SASC or other members of the Senate can lose trust in the ability of the Services and DoD to nominate exemplary officers. Past breaches of trust have resulted in public hearings, lack of confirmation of nominees, increased scrutiny of future nominees, and increased legislation regarding Service and DoD processes.

---

[1] The HASC does not have the authority to confirm officer nominations. However, it does oversee DoD through the annual passage of the NDAA (in conjunction with the Senate) and through oversight hearings. A recent example of a relevant HASC hearing is "Senior Leader Misconduct: Prevention and Accountability" (Fine, 2018).

[2] For more-specific details on the jurisdiction of the SASC, see U.S. Senate Committee on Armed Services, "History," webpage, undated a. The U.S. Space Force is not addressed in this report because it was established on December 20, 2019, when the project was approaching completion.

This chapter is particularly informed by meetings with SASC professional staff, although meetings with DoD and Service representatives also were relevant. The SASC staff members bring to bear decades of experience working with senators on the officer confirmation process, learning about Senate concerns regarding adverse and reportable information reporting practices, and meeting with senior Service and DoD representatives on these matters. The SASC staff with whom we met included individuals who had provided information for the 2010 RAND review.

Senate Armed Services Committee Review Process

Once the President has approved the nomination (or nominations) provided by DoD, the White House Clerk is responsible for forwarding the nomination scroll to the Senate Clerk.[3] At that point, G/FO Matters directs the Services to provide the hard-copy personnel package binders containing the adverse or reportable information to the SASC nominations clerk.[4] These binders include the information described at the beginning of Chapter Three, such as the report of investigation and the complete investigation materials, all of which DoD will have already reviewed.

G/FO Matters then sends a letter to the chairman of the SASC, attaching the adverse information summary, the reportable information summary, or both. The SASC staff reviews the nomination packages for completeness. The staff members read every document in the files to which they are assigned, and these files can be hundreds of pages long. If any information is missing, the SASC staff requests additional information from DoD or the Services. Additionally, at times, senators would like to review material that, as a general rule, is not required to be submitted, such as adverse information that the SASC had previously reviewed. In those cases, requests for this type of information are made by an exception, not a change in overall SASC expectations for all packages. If the SASC contacts the Service directly about adverse or reportable information, the Service can respond directly so long as it coordinates the response with G/FO Matters.[5] If the Service is unable to coordinate with G/FO Matters before providing additional information to the SASC, the Service must provide G/FO Matters with copies "of any written inquiries and responses or summaries of any verbal communications."[6]

Once the SASC staff members have reviewed a nomination package, they verbally brief (without slides) members of the SASC and help answer questions about the package contents. The SASC staff does not search the internet for information on officers; however, events or allegations involving officers that receive significant media coverage will come to the Senate's attention. The SASC staff routinely coordinates with DoD on the status of nominations, holds, additional information needs, prioritization of files, and other aspects of the process.

The SASC rules allow members of the SASC one week to review the nominations and raise any issues regarding nominees.[7] The list of nominees is also posted to the Senate's public

---

[3]   DoDI 1320.04, 2014, p. 14.

[4]   DoDI 1320.04, 2014, p. 15.

[5]   DoDI 1320.04, 2014, p. 15.

[6]   DoDI 1320.04, 2014, p. 15.

[7]   U.S. Senate Committee on Armed Services, "Rules of Procedure," webpage, undated c.

website as a public notice function, and sometimes, as a result, a member of the public will raise a concern with a senator. The SASC votes on nominations once a month. A quorum of SASC members must be present to move a nomination out of committee. SASC staff report that almost all nominees reported out of committee to the full Senate will have obtained the unanimous consent of the SASC members. Once the nomination is reported out of committee, Senate rules require that the nomination be on the Senate floor for at least one full day before a full vote.

The Senate typically votes at the very end of the month to ensure that the vote includes all officer nominations that in that month are within 120 days of promotion or appointment, as well as to ensure that any officers with promotion or appointment dates at the beginning of the next month are confirmed in time. After the nomination moves to a full vote, it takes only one senator to hold a nomination. If a senator places a hold on a nomination, it is the responsibility of the Service to coordinate with the senator to address the issues or concerns to move the nomination forward. SASC staff report that, in many cases, a senator prefers to speak directly to the Service leadership or the nominee before placing an affirmative vote.

Overall, SASC staff report that existing DoD policies and processes are working to meet SASC expectations for adverse and reportable information reporting practices. The updated policy (DoDI 1320.04) provides more-detailed definitions, instructions, and timelines designed to meet the SASC's requirements.

Timelines

Certain time limitations apply to Senate action on a nomination. Nominations cannot be submitted to the Senate more than nine months prior to the projected date of promotion or appointment. The SASC will act on pending nominations within four months of the projected date of promotion or assignment.[8] The Senate does not wish to vote far in advance, because once a nomination is confirmed, it cannot be rescinded, even if new allegations against the officer come to light. This practice might limit the officer's leadership preparation between confirmation and assumption of new duties.[9] SASC staff report that review of packages containing adverse or reportable information will necessitate a voting delay of at least a month because it takes time to review the information, and the Senate confirms nominations once a month. Depending on the complexity of the case, the delay can extend to two to three months. Furthermore, nominations will not be acted upon when Congress is in recess for more than 30 days or at the end of a session of Congress. Any packages submitted during a recess will be returned to OSD through the White House. Given competing priorities and the length of some of the adverse and reportable information files, at times the Senate is unable to vote on a nomination before it expires. SASC staff report that, if alerted, they can prioritize reviews for time-intensive files with adverse or reportable information.

---

[8]   DoDI 1320.04, 2014, p. 14.

[9]   For example, research indicates that officers appointed as superintendents of the military service academies require a minimum of four months of preparation after confirmation and before assuming command but are typically afforded only one to three months of preparation time between confirmation and assumption of command. See William A. Chambers, Joseph F. Adams, William R. Burns, Jr., Kathleen M. Conley, Rachel D. Dubin, and Waldo D. Freeman, *Review of the Roles, Selection, and Evaluation of Superintendents of the Military Service Academies*, Alexandria, Va.: Institute for Defense Analyses, P-5219, December 2014.

Confidentiality of Requested Adverse and Reportable Information

SASC staff described how the SASC safeguards adverse and reportable information documents to guard against leaks. First, the SASC minimizes access to this information, limiting access to the files to four trusted, experienced, professional staff members. The staff works with only the single paper copy files of the documents, and those files are returned to DoD after actions are complete. Any of the professional staff members' own notes are destroyed. The SASC professional staff work directly with SASC members; they do not interact with senators' personal staff on these issues. The SASC does not save the information to the Senate files. SASC staff told us that sometimes an officer under consideration will contact a senator asking why the nomination package appears to be held up, and the senator's staff makes inquiries on the officer's behalf. This can result in calling attention to the officer's adverse or reportable information, which otherwise would not have warranted being elevated to such a degree.

The SASC requires unredacted investigation files for review for the confirmation process because the narrative can be very difficult to follow when all names and other identifying information have been redacted. As noted earlier, some of the offices that produce these files are concerned that sharing unredacted copies risks compromising the IG system with regard to protecting victims, witnesses, and whistleblowers and the willingness of individuals to make reports that could end up before senators.

Topics of Senate Interest

The SASC does not maintain or provide DoD with a standing list of issues it considers to be reportable because of ongoing Senate priorities and interests. There are some well-known categories of reportable information (detainee abuse, friendly fire, and others), but one SASC staff member used a functional test to describe additional reportable information: information that a constituent might ask a senator about in connection with the senator's confirmation vote. Even if the officer did nothing wrong, the Senate will want to be aware of the officer's potential association with these events so that members can respond to constituent concerns if necessary. The Senate also might consider whether the leader can be effective in the proposed assignment given an association with a controversial event.

Adverse and Reportable Information Summaries

SASC staff read all of the adverse and reportable information contained in the personnel packages, including investigative reports and their supporting documents. The staff noted that sometimes Service summaries of adverse or reportable information do not summarize all of the unfavorable information. The staff also noted that some summaries appear to advocate for the officer by minimizing allegations and emphasizing mitigating factors. However, the summaries are supposed to be neutral and factual and reflect all adverse and reportable information. When the secretaries of the military departments submit personnel action packages for officers with adverse or reportable information, they must justify how and why the officer merits the appointment or promotion despite that unfavorable information.[10] Summaries that do not provide an accurate sense of the officer's adverse or reportable information do a disservice to those secretaries, and this can become particularly noticeable in meetings with SASC members to discuss a nominee.

---

[10] DoDI 1320.04, 2014, p. 11.

Misconduct in the Military Context

SASC staff explained that senators had encountered concerns from military leaders that the SASC or members of the Senate might not understand or fully appreciate the military context of actions or decisionmaking on the battlefield. The fear is that the Senate will fail to confirm well-qualified officers with solid careers whose undesirable behavior occurred solely under stressful and threatening circumstances. The SASC staff clarified that for some types of cases the SASC does discuss the context of misconduct; however, the battlefield context does not explain why officers would later lie about their actions, destroy evidence, fail to report incidents, or refuse to cooperate with investigations. These subsequent actions, outside the "heat of the battle," can lead members of the SASC to question the integrity of the officer. There have been cases in which the officer would have been confirmable if they had accepted responsibility for the original behavior, but the lack of integrity made the confirmation untenable.

New Congressional Requirements for Promotion Boards

As referenced in Chapter Three, Section 502 of the FY 2020 NDAA expanded the requirement for furnishing adverse information on officers to selection boards. Adverse information already had to be provided to selection boards considering promotions to O-7 and above, but such information for the lower pay grades was not sought until after the promotion selection boards had made their selections for promotion, and this information was sought only for those already selected. Then, promotion review boards would review the adverse information and recommend, based on consideration of the individual, whether to promote—rather than weighing the officer's record according to the context of the broader pool.

The revised law now requires furnishing adverse information to boards considering active-component promotions to O-4 and above and reserve-component promotions to O-6 and above.[11] Furthermore, the new statutory provision requires furnishing adverse information at every phase of consideration thereafter. Notably, the language in the provision requires the furnishing of *adverse*, but not *reportable*, information to the boards; however, the distinction in terms is one in DoDI 1320.04 rather than Title 10 of the U.S. Code.

Although the provision became effective when the FY 2020 NDAA was enacted (December 20, 2019), the Services expressed concerns about the feasibility of performing these checks with existing funding and workforce allocations. The major issue at hand is the order of magnitude of work that the changes require. Postboard adverse information checks reduced the workload by necessitating searching for adverse information for only the subset of officers already selected rather than the entire pool under consideration. The population of officers being considered for promotion to the grades of O-4 through O-6 is significantly larger than the population being considered for promotion to the grades of O-7 through O-10 (i.e., thousands of officers versus hundreds). As an example of the implications, the U.S. Navy indicated that, by its own estimates, the changes (as proposed in the Senate draft of the bill that was public at the time of our interviews) would require five to six times the labor, at a minimum. The Services further indicated that additional requirements would increase the workload not only for the offices that manage the personnel processes but also for those that must perform the database checks (such as the IG and EEO offices). DoD, the Services, and the SASC share

---

[11] Pub. L. 116-92, 2019.

an interest in ensuring that officers meet the requirement for exemplary conduct as laid forth in Title 10 of the U.S. Code. However, the Services reported that their data systems and workforce at the time of our study were insufficient to meet the new requirements, and thus major adjustments would need to be made.

Senate Armed Services Committee Questionnaire for O-9 and O-10 Nominations

One specific vehicle for reporting information is the SASC questionnaire, required for officers nominated to O-9 and O-10. The questionnaire is completed by the officer after the military department secretary has submitted the officer's personnel package and concurrently with any CJSC review. It provides background information used by the Senate during the confirmation process. The questionnaire asks about basic biographical information that will be made public, including government experience and business relationships. The questionnaire further asks nominees to commit to the "furtherance of Congressional oversight," including a commitment to testify before the SASC and its subcommittees; to provide personal views, even if their views differ from an administration; and to provide appropriate materials to the SASC and SASC staff when asked. The questionnaire requires nominees to provide a financial disclosure and list any potential conflicts of interest. The officer is asked to self-report on any legal matters, including any disciplinary action for unprofessional behavior; any current or former investigations, arrests, or charges by federal, state, or local authorities; and whether the officer or the officer's spouse has any ties to foreign entities. The questionnaire that we reviewed also provides officers with an opportunity to raise any issues that they believe might affect their nominations: "Please advise the Committee of any additional information, favorable or unfavorable, which you feel should be considered in connection with your nomination."[12]

Interviews with relevant Service, DoD, and SASC representatives indicate a few challenges regarding the SASC questionnaire. First, it is possible for officers to have been under investigation but be unaware of this fact and therefore respond that they have not ever been investigated. This can happen in cases in which the complaints were dismissed as frivolous or not credible, and not notifying the officers protects them from accusations of retaliation if they later give the complainants poor performance evaluations or discipline them for legitimate reasons. In this way, officers' SASC questionnaire responses could conflict with other material included in the personnel package. The second challenge is that information can come to light through the SASC questionnaire that can surprise the Service and the CJCS because they had not been aware of it previously. An officer's response to a question about having *ever* been investigated can reveal information that had appropriately been excluded from the personnel package because of the age of the information or previous Senate review of it. Depending on how common or serious these issues have been, the Services might wish to consider having officers complete the questionnaire at an earlier point in the process so that the Services can manage any new information that it reveals and potentially address this information in the secretary's memo.

---

[12]   U.S. Senate Committee on Armed Services, 116th Congress, "Senate Armed Services Questionnaire: Information Requested of Nominees for Certain Senior Military Positions," undated, p. 8, version provided to the authors by the research sponsor on June 13, 2019.

Summary

The SASC, DoD, and the Services share a desire to promote the best qualified officers, and identifying adverse or reportable information is important for determining whether those officers have demonstrated exemplary conduct. Although the SASC requires that nomination packages include summaries of adverse and reportable information, it also wants to receive the most-complete information, including unredacted investigation files, comprehensive answers to the SASC questionnaire, and, in some cases, information beyond the scope of the ten-year window for adverse information and the three-year window for certain types of reportable information. The 2014 update to the DoDI provided more-detailed definitions of adverse and reportable information and reporting requirements that are more aligned with SASC expectations.

CHAPTER SEVEN

Key Findings and Recommendations

This chapter summarizes the research findings on the management of military officer adverse and reportable information and provides corresponding recommendations. As noted in Chapters Three through Seven, updates to DoD and Service policies since the 2010 RAND review provide more-explicit guidance and greater standardization in reporting from across the Services. However, several opportunities exist to address new and remaining gaps, ambiguities, and inconsistencies. We make several recommendations for OSD and the Services to consider to clarify the processes for using adverse and reportable information in regard to military officer appointments, assignments, promotions, and retirements. This information is also provided in the report's Summary.

Key Findings

The study had several key findings regarding the processes for reporting adverse and reportable information, inconsistencies among the Services in how policies are applied, and concerns voiced by the SASC.

Policy Definitions and Reporting Requirements

The updated 2014 policy offers more detail and clarity on definitions of adverse and reportable information and reporting requirements, but some ambiguity remains. For example, it is unclear whether the Services should be conducting internet searches to identify officers connected with significant events widely known to the general public that meet the reportable information threshold and, if so, what search criteria are expected. Furthermore, the policy is not explicit on whether the adverse information definition intentionally excluded probable cause information, a lower threshold of proof than preponderance of the evidence. Also, there is variation in Service understandings of the phrase "investigation or inquiry," with some offices delineating an intake or pre-investigation phase in which a complaint has been received but the office is still verifying elements of the allegation (e.g., which individual is being accused) and deciding whether to open a formal investigation. Trust with the Senate can be eroded when members learn after a vote that the Services were aware of an open allegation against an officer but did not report it in time for the Senate's consideration.

The definition of *adverse* in DoDI 1320.04 permits the exclusion of incidents that resulted in no more than nonpunitive rehabilitative counseling. Different superior officers may choose different courses of action in response to the same behavior. Thus, the language in the definition introduces opportunities for inconsistent reporting of adverse information across officers and across Services, because the policy permits behaviors to be reported as adverse for some officers but not for others on the basis of the type of action their superiors took.

Personnel Processes

The 2014 policy outlining the personnel action processes built upon and expanded the previous 1995 DoDI in multiple ways. The new policy integrates guidance that had been published in several memoranda subsequent to the 1995 policy, such as those regarding G/FO retirements. The 2014 DoDI expands responsibility for ensuring policy compliance, which now falls not only to the USD(P&R) but also to the secretaries of the military departments and the CJCS.

The revised policy also more clearly documents the responsibilities of the Services, Departments, and Joint Chiefs for managing the officer personnel packages. It explicitly lists the records that the Services must check for adverse and reportable information for personnel actions for officers in pay grades O-7 and above, requires that the military department secretaries certify that those checks have been completed, and specifies when those checks must be updated. The new policy also specifies that the CJCS will review and comment on all G/FO promotions, nominations, and retirement packages containing adverse or reportable information.

The 2014 DoDI also contains a new enclosure (Enclosure 6) on the reporting requirements for personnel actions for officers in the grades of O-6 and below. The enclosure does not require that the same list of records be systematically checked for officers in pay grades O-6 and below,[1] because reporting adverse and reportable information for these officers is not universally required. The new policy explains the exceptions where reporting this information for officers in these pay grades is required, such as when the information has received significant media or SASC attention or when the military department secretaries deem it appropriate to include.

The separate policy that focuses on cross-Service and cross-component transfers, DoDI 1300.04, requires concurrence by both the gaining Service and the losing Service but does not discuss adverse or reportable information or exemplary conduct and does not reference DoDI 1320.04.[2] DoD guidance on the original appointment of officers,[3] DoDI 1310.02, does indicate that the procedures in DoDI 1320.04 should be followed for adverse and reportable information, but that original appointments policy does not include a transfers section focused on the timing and extent of adverse or reportable information that the losing Service or component should provide to the gaining one.[4] No policy appears to contain a complete, integrated list of the transfer-specific procedures regarding adverse and reportable information.

The processes for identifying, reviewing, and reporting adverse and reportable information are labor-intensive and time-consuming and require coordination across many offices. In speaking with these offices, we heard repeatedly about good working relationships across many organizations that help staff with judgment calls on complicated situations, questions about

---

[1] Officers in the pay grade of O-6 who are up for promotion to O-7, the first G/FO pay grade, are the exception because they are considered senior officials and are held to the higher standard.

[2] DoDI 1300.04, 2017.

[3] Transfers require an original appointment by the gaining Service or component.

[4] DoDI 1310.02, 2015.

policy interpretation or application, and status updates as the officers' personnel action packages move through different stages.

Recent developments include the FY 2019 NDAA authorizing officers who have open investigations of misconduct to conditionally retire, which provides the option to revisit the retirement pay grade upon the conclusion of the investigation. Thus, in cases in which it appears highly unlikely that allegations against the retiring officers will be substantiated, the officers and their families can be permitted to move forward and to access retirement benefits rather than waiting months or even years for the investigations to conclude. Also, in December 2019, as this research project was ending, the FY 2020 NDAA was approved, mandating that adverse information now be furnished to additional promotion selection boards (boards considering promotion to O-4 and above for active-component officers and to O-6 and above for reserve-component officers rather than just to boards considering promotion to G/FO ranks). In responding to earlier draft legislation on this topic, the Services reported that their allocated resources for these processes at that time was seriously inadequate for the additional workload. Thus, significant efforts will need to be undertaken for implementation, and the new requirements will need to be integrated into a revision of DoDI 1320.04.

Sources of Adverse and Reportable Information

Potential sources of adverse and reportable information are located within and outside DoD. Sources that must be checked for G/FO personnel actions are now listed in the 2014 policy, DoDI 1320.04. Among those explicitly named are the MEO and EEO files, which the previous RAND assessment had found were not both being consistently checked, because some staff were not aware of the distinction.[5]

One policy compliance challenge is that the FBI's NCIC database cannot be checked as required by DoD policy, because authorization is limited to only law enforcement agencies for law enforcement purposes.

Service offices have benefited from upgrades to their systems for checking sources for adverse and reportable information; however, some database and workforce limitations present significant and persistent obstacles to moving these packages through the processes in a timely manner. For example, search functions that require manual entry of each officer's name and that require the name to exactly match that in any unseen record make an inefficient use of military personnel and can still fail to locate existing files. The FY 2020 NDAA requires data checks on even more and significantly larger groups of officers, which increases those workforce demands. Without improvements to such data systems, the Services will have an increased demand on their workforce to meet the new requirement, or the thoroughness of the data checks might be compromised, or there could be a backlog in conducting these checks that keeps some officers' records from being completed on time. Delays in checking data sources and completing investigations can create more opportunities or incentives for valued officers to leave military service rather than wait for the delayed promotion or assignment decisions. Delays can also result in gaps in filling leadership positions or some positions being filled by less qualified officers. Additionally, drawn-out, unresolved investigations of allegations against officers can undermine the reputation and authority of these officers and cause potentially lasting damage, even for officers who are ultimately exonerated.

---

[5] As noted earlier, MEO files track complaints by military personnel, while EEO files track complaints by civilian employees.

Even though many databases are checked for adverse or reportable information, some databases, such as professional license investigation records or the employee records of National Guard and reserve officers who are also DoD civilian employees, are not explicitly required to be checked. Note, however, that some information gaps are inevitable. For example, some allegations are made only after an officer becomes a prominent nominee for a G/FO rank or position, and some information sources would be impractical to pursue (such as the nongovernmental civilian employment records of guard and reserve officers).

The Service headquarters have differing levels of access to unfavorable information found in CDIs, as a result, that information is not consistently reported in officer personnel action packages. Headquarters-level Service process requirements range from tracking all CDIs into officers as soon as they are opened (Air Force and Marine Corps), to tracking only substantiated adverse findings for officers in grades O-4 and above after the investigations are completed (Army), to having no centralized tracking of CDIs at all (Navy). These differences put some officers who were investigated by their commander at a career disadvantage compared with their peers in other Services. Services lacking a centralized database with complete CDI information risk clearing a nominee who might in fact have adverse or reportable information that will come to light at a later point in the confirmation process.

U.S. Department of Defense and Senate Armed Services Committee Practices and Perspectives

The Services and DoD will never review officer files with the exact same lens as the SASC. The additional information presented in DoDI 1320.04 in 2014 better aligns both DoD policy and practice with SASC expectations by providing more-specific definitions, reporting requirements, and guidance on personnel processes that reflect SASC intentions; for example, the new policy is specific about which data sources should be checked. However, different perspectives and approaches to managing adverse and reportable information still exist and can be the source of some SASC dissatisfaction with certain personnel action packages that it receives and, in turn, some Service or DoD surprise at SASC requests or actions.

SASC staff emphasized that senators evaluate adverse and reportable information in personnel packages according to not only whether allegations of officers violating rules or laws were substantiated but also whether the officers displayed integrity, good leadership, and sound judgment. An officer could be cleared of an allegation, yet other behavior documented in the investigation could cause the SASC to question whether the officer is suitable for a greater level of trust, authority, and responsibility. Thus, investigation information from unsubstantiated allegations might need to be reported in such cases.

Additionally, SASC staff reported that some summaries of adverse or reportable information were written to be persuasive on the officer's behalf by minimizing the allegations, emphasizing mitigating factors, and describing the actions taken by a command in response to a behavior; however, the SASC expects the summaries to be neutral and factual, reflect all adverse and reportable information, and demonstrate that the military department secretaries and Service Chiefs were provided with an accurate sense of the officers they are endorsing for appointment, promotion, or assignment. In contrast to the factual summary, the military department secretary's separate memorandum is where leadership is expected to make a persuasive argument that the officer meets the exemplary conduct standards described in Title 10 and explain why the officer's personnel action is being supported despite the adverse information.

Where to draw the line on what information to report is a source of ongoing discussion and concern. OSD and the Services are trying to apply guidance on what to include and exclude. Their efforts require coordination across several offices, must be completed within a set timeline, and sometimes require several thick binders of documents per officer. There is no established list of SASC items of current interest that must be reported, although some are well known through experience (e.g., any association with a unit investigated for detainee abuse). SASC staff highlighted a preference for the Services erring on the side of providing more-complete information yet also affirmed that some limits are desirable given the volume of documents that must be reviewed. Although SASC staff confirmed that the policy appropriately limits the reporting of adverse information to allegations received in the past ten years or that have not been previously reviewed by the SASC, in some cases the SASC will request information that goes beyond those limits. Additionally, a SASC questionnaire for O-9 and O-10 nominees asks them to self-report *ever* having been the subject of a previous complaint, which is a request for responses not bounded by a certain period of years, a previous Senate review, or a threshold of only allegations that had been substantiated.

SASC staff noted that officers have expressed and occasionally acted upon fears that the presence of any adverse or reportable information in a nomination package will automatically disqualify them from confirmation; however, that is not the case. Staff emphasized that senators want to be aware of and understand the circumstances under which an incident or complaint might arise so that they can make informed decisions and address any questions that might come from their constituents. But SASC, DoD, and Service representatives with whom we met wanted to ensure that commanders do not fail to take appropriate action with subordinates or document unfavorable information as required based on assumptions that doing so would eliminate the possibility for those subordinates to advance at the senior level.

For Further Study

Additional common themes raised during our study merit consideration for further study, since we had insufficient data to evaluate them. We heard repeated concerns that complaints against officers are being "weaponized," or reported at strategic moments simply to derail officers' careers. Further study would be needed to understand the nature, extent, or impact of such a phenomenon, if it does indeed exist. Additionally, the full impact of the timeline necessary to process personnel packages containing adverse or reportable information is not well documented. For example, what is the impact on the individual officers, their relationships, their authority, and their ability to lead while facing open allegations? What is the impact on their career opportunities and their motivation to remain in the military? Do unresolved allegations against leaders have an impact on the morale and cohesion of their units? Moreover, what is the risk to subordinates of drawn-out investigations when the officers who have engaged in misconduct remain in positions of authority until the investigation is closed? The point is that the processes we are describing are not just bureaucratic but are ones whose real costs and benefits depend on how they are executed.

Recommendations

We make several recommendations for OSD and the Services to consider to clarify the processes for using adverse and reportable information regarding military officer appointments, assignments, promotions, and retirements. Some recommendations are less specific than others because the DoD Adverse and Reportable Information Working Group will be convening to deliberate details necessary for any changes to be adopted.

Policy Definitions and Reporting Requirements

Recommendations regarding policy definitions and reporting requirements are as follows:

- **OSD should further refine the adverse and reportable information definitions and reporting requirements to address ambiguities in DoDI 1320.04 and align DoD and Senate requirements.** For example, the policy should clarify when information from unsubstantiated allegations might need to be reported; whether probable cause is a standard that meets the adverse information threshold; that OEPM should be notified immediately of new allegations against an officer with a pending personnel action (rather than after completion of an intake or pre-investigation phase); and whether DoD or the SASC expects internet searches for adverse or reportable information for any of the personnel processes and, if so, what search guidelines should be used.
- **OSD should remove from the adverse information criteria the language stating that the level or type of a superior's disciplinary action in response to an officer's behavior should in part determine whether substantiated allegations are adverse information that should be reported.** Responses to a given behavior can vary across commanders, and commanders might respond differently for different officers. DoDI 1320.04's definition of *adverse* permits the exclusion of incidents that resulted in no more than nonpunitive rehabilitative counseling; this definition introduces opportunities for inconsistent reporting of adverse information across officers and Services. The policy permits behaviors to be reported as adverse for some officers but not for others on the basis of the type of action their superiors took. Removing that possibility for exclusion would contribute to more-consistent reporting practices within and across the Services.

Personnel Processes

Recommendations regarding personnel processes are as follows:

- **OSD and the Services should sustain and extend the positive aspects of current processes,** such as modernizing data systems, maintaining good relationships and communication across organizations, and maintaining data safeguarding measures to prevent leaks and maintain the integrity of personnel processes.
- **OSD should detail in policy the adverse and reportable information reporting requirements and processes for officers seeking cross-Service and cross-component transfers.** DoD's reporting expectations regarding officers leaving one Service or component and requesting an appointment to another are not well documented in policy. Gaps in reporting by the losing Services or components leave the gaining Services or components vulnerable to unknowingly accepting officers with behaviors that kept them from being promoted or retained in their original Service or component. Because DoDI 1320.04 has become the central reference for the management of adverse and reportable information regarding military officers, DoD might wish to retitle the policy and include the person-

nel actions for which DoD has oversight, but DoDI 1300.04 should also be updated to mention the transfer of adverse and reportable information.

Sources of Adverse and Reportable Information

Recommendations regarding sources of adverse and reportable information are as follows:

- **OSD and the Services should invest in data systems and personnel dedicated to these processes to ensure that the data checks are as complete and accurate as possible, and that the packages proceed in an efficient and timely manner.** Offices involved in checking for and reporting adverse and reportable information explained how database search technology limitations and limited staffing relative to the workload present hurdles to meeting the accurate reporting and timeline requirements. Additionally, new FY 2020 NDAA requirements dramatically increase the data check workload; adverse information must be provided to boards deliberating on active-component officer promotions to O-4 and above and reserve-component officer promotions to O-6 and above, not just to boards considering promotions to O-7 and above. Previously, the workload for promotions to O-6 and below was smaller; searches for adverse and reportable information were conducted *after* the boards and only for the subset of officers who had already been selected. At the Service level, an examination of all of the legal reviews conducted throughout the process could reveal opportunities for greater efficiency or swifter processing if quality legal reviews do not require as many reviewers.
- **OSD should require changes to remedy the lack of standardization among the Services regarding headquarters-level access to information from CDIs and monitor for compliance.** Standardization is important for equity for officers across the Services and for Service competition for joint leadership positions. Additionally, the law states that DoD regulations governing information furnished to selection boards shall apply uniformly among the military departments.[6] The Air Force and Marine Corps policies and processes give centralized access to CDI information, but the U.S. Navy does not have an equivalent and the Army has only partial access. Thus, officers who are the subject of open CDIs in the U.S. Navy or the Army could have personnel actions moving forward that would be held back if those officers were in the Air Force or the Marine Corps. Additionally, Army processes diverge from processes of DoD and other Services by instructing IGs to delete officers' names from the subject/suspect fields in their IG database when closing out cases for completed CDIs that began as a complaint to the IG.
- **OSD should update DoDI 1320.04 to remove the required check of the FBI's NCIC database for G/FO personnel actions, since it is not an authorized use of this database, and indicate any replacement.** The NCIC is permitted for law enforcement purposes only, not for employment activities. Moreover, it covers only current "hot" cases, such as wanted persons, missing persons, and suspected terrorists, rather than criminal history. A potential alternative to the NCIC is the FBI's NGI System, which tracks criminal history and can be used for employment purposes if certain authorization and technical requirements are met. Alternatively, the new Trusted Workforce 2.0 security clearance continuous vetting process might meet OSD's and the SASC's needs for recent criminal database checks.

---

[6]   10 U.S.C. 615(a) and 14107(a).

- **OSD should consider whether additional data sources—such as professional license or privilege investigations records or the civilian employee records for guard and reserve officers who are also DoD civilian employees—should be checked for adverse or reportable information.** The record-checking requirements are already numerous and labor-intensive to meet, and some information gaps will always exist because some sources are inaccessible or impractical to search. However, it might be feasible and prudent to check additional data sources for all or a subset of officer personnel actions. For example, DoD might wish to explore the value, legality, and feasibility of considering whether the civilian personnel files of guard and reserve officers who are also DoD civilian employees contain unfavorable information that is not reflected in some manner in their military records. Additionally, for officers in certain careers, it might be practical to require a systematic check for professional license or privilege investigations (e.g., for medical or legal malpractice).
- **The Services should prepare a user-friendly officer's guide** on adverse and reportable information definitions, reporting requirements, and procedures. Officers make critical decisions about how or whether to record and report adverse and reportable information through performance reviews, disciplinary letters, CDIs, and other actions. Their decisions can determine whether crucial information is visible or hidden during personnel action processes. The policy (DoDI 1320.04) is necessarily legalistic. Service-specific officers' guides should advise officers on how and why this type of information must be recorded, shared, and used and reference the Service, DoD, and legal requirements. The guide should also clarify that the Senate does not automatically reject personnel actions for officers who have adverse information; SASC staff estimate that more than 90 percent of such nominations are confirmed. Actual examples based on officers with adverse and reportable behavior could be illustrative, including how officers overcame early career missteps and how concealment of such information can be worse than the original problem. To promote compliance, each Service's guide should address DoD and Service expectations about recording and reporting information from CDIs and MEO investigations. The Services should consider making their guides a mandatory part of commanders' courses, beginning at the O-4 level, as well as mandatory for personnel involved in the processes (e.g., the IGs).

U.S. Department of Defense and Senate Armed Services Committee Practices and Perspectives

Recommendations regarding DoD and SASC practices and perspectives are as follows:

- **G/FO Matters should discuss with the DoD and Service IG offices potential options to address IG concerns about requirements to include unredacted investigation files in personnel action packages for the SASC. If an alternative is feasible and the SASC approves, G/FO Matters should formalize any new requirements through policy.** Because the SASC does not have full confidence that the adverse and reportable information summaries are sufficiently accurate and comprehensive, the SASC requires complete investigation files, including exhibits and submitted statements, to be provided for its review. Unredacted versions are required because redacted narratives can be difficult or impossible to follow. The IGs are obligated to comply but also to protect whistleblowers and to preserve the integrity of open investigations and the IG system that relies upon individuals to report violations and cooperate in investigations. OSD should explore with the IGs whether there are alternative approaches that might meet SASC expectations for information-sharing and reader comprehension while protecting the identity of whistle-blowers, victims, and witnesses.

- **OSD and the Services should provide guidance and training to the responsible individuals on how to prepare neutral, factual, and complete adverse and reportable information summaries that meet SASC expectations.** SASC staff emphasized that these summaries should not be persuasive arguments on the officer's behalf. This summary format will help ensure that the Service Chiefs and the secretaries of the military departments are fully aware of the adverse and reportable information, since, unlike the SASC staff, they likely will not read the full investigative files. Improvements to information summaries will also better serve the military department secretaries: Adverse and reportable information must be described in the memoranda with enough context to demonstrate that they are completely aware of the specific substantiated adverse information or have a full understanding of the reportable information when they endorse officers as meeting the exemplary conduct standards. An overview of these recommendations and related findings is presented in Table 7.1.

Table 7.1
Overview of Recommendations and Related Findings

Recommended For	Recommendation	Related Finding
Policy definitions and reporting requirements		
OSD	Refine the adverse and reportable information definitions and reporting requirements to address ambiguities in DoDI 1320.04 and align DoD and Senate requirements.	Ambiguity in definitions and reporting requirements remain in DoDI 1320.04.
OSD	Revisit whether the level or type of a superior's disciplinary action in response to an officer's behavior should in part determine whether substantiated allegations are adverse information that should be reported.	DoDI 1320.04's definition of *adverse* permits the exclusion of incidents that received no more than nonpunitive rehabilitative counseling, introducing opportunities for inconsistent reporting across officers and Services depending on how superiors respond.
Personnel processes		
OSD and the Services	Sustain and further extend the positive aspects of current processes.	The success of adverse and reportable information processes depends on coordination across many offices.
OSD	The update to DoDI 1320.04 should detail the adverse and reportable information reporting requirements and processes for officers seeking cross-Service or cross-component transfers.	No single policy contains an integrated list of transfer-specific procedures regarding adverse and reportable information.
Sources of adverse and reportable information		
OSD and the Services	Invest in data systems and personnel dedicated to these processes to promote data check completeness and accuracy and to ensure that packages proceed more quickly and efficiently.	Technological and staffing limitations present challenges to meeting accurate reporting and timeline requirements.
OSD	Require changes to remedy the lack of standardization among the Services regarding headquarters-level access to information from CDIs and monitor for compliance.	Service headquarters have different levels of access to and thus reporting of information found in CDIs, putting some officers at a career disadvantage compared with their peers in other Services.
OSD	Update DoDI 1320.04 to remove the required check of the FBI's NCIC database for G/FO personnel actions, and indicate any replacement.	The NCIC database cannot be checked for personnel actions as required by DoD policy, because authorization is limited to only law enforcement agencies for law enforcement purposes.
OSD	Consider whether additional data sources should be checked for adverse and reportable information.	Additional data sources exist that could be checked for adverse or reportable information.
The Services	Consider preparing a user-friendly officer's guide on adverse and reportable information definitions, reporting requirements, and procedures.	Inconsistencies in individual reporting decisions can determine whether crucial information is visible or hidden during personnel action processes.

Table 7.1—Continued

Recommended For	Recommendation	Related Finding
DoD and SASC practices and perspectives		
G/FO Matters	Discuss with DoD and the Service IG offices IG concerns about requirements to include unredacted investigation files in personnel packages for the SASC. Explore whether alternative approaches might meet SASC expectations and IG concerns.	The SASC requires complete, unredacted investigation files. The Service IGs are obligated to comply but also to protect whistleblowers and preserve the integrity of open investigations and the IG system more broadly.
OSD and the Services	Provide guidance and training to the responsible individuals on how to prepare adverse and reportable information summaries that meet SASC expectations.	The SASC expects neutral, factual summaries reflecting all adverse and reportable information, while the Services at times provide persuasive summaries written to advocate for the officer. The military department secretary's memo is where the persuasive case is to be made.

List of Key U.S. Department of Defense and Service Policies and Guidance Consulted

For our research, we collected historical and existing policies potentially relevant for our analysis. Although some policies are cited throughout the body of the report, the more comprehensive list is provided in this appendix.

U.S. Department of Defense

Assistant Secretary of Defense for Force Management Policy, "Processing Three- and Four-Star Retirement Requests," memorandum for Acting Secretary of the Army, Acting Secretary of the Navy, Acting Secretary of the Air Force, Chairman of the Joint Chiefs of Staff, Washington, D.C., May 21, 2001.

Assistant Secretary of Defense for Force Management Policy, "Interim Change to Department of Defense Instruction (DoDI) 1320.4, 'Military Officer Actions Requiring Approval of the Secretary of Defense or President, or Confirmation by the Senate,'" memorandum for Secretary of the Army, Secretary of the Navy, Secretary of the Air Force, Chairman of the Joint Chiefs of Staff, Washington, D.C., February 27, 2002.

DoD, *The DoD Civilian Equal Employment Opportunity (EEO) Program*, DoDD 1440.1, May 21, 1987, Administrative Reissuance Incorporating Through Change 3, April 17, 1992.

DoD, *Military Officer Actions Requiring Approval of the Secretary of Defense or the President, or Confirmation by the Senate*, DoDI 1320.4, March 14, 1995.

DoD, *Defense Industrial Personnel Security Clearance Review Program*, DoDD 5220.6, January 2, 1992, Administrative Reissuance Incorporating Through Change 4, April 20, 1999.

DoD, *Initiation of Investigations by Military Criminal Investigative Organizations*, DoDI 5505.3, June 21, 2002.

DoD, *Principal Deputy Under Secretary of Defense for Personnel and Readiness (PDUSD(P&R))*, DoDD 5124.8, July 16, 2003.

DoD, *Investigations of Allegations Against Senior Officials of the Department of Defense*, DoDD 5505.06, April 10, 2006.

DoD, *Standards of Conduct*, DoDD 5500.07, November 29, 2007.

DoD, *Joint Ethics Regulation*, DoDD 5500.07-R, August 30, 1993, Incorporating Change 7, November 11, 2011.

DoD, *Investigations of Allegations Against Senior DoD Officials*, DoDD 5505.06, June 6, 2013.

DoD, *Medical Quality Assurance (MQA) and Clinical Quality Management in the Military Health Care System (MHS)*, DoDM 6025.13, October 29, 2013.

DoD, *Military Officer Actions Requiring Presidential, Secretary of Defense, or Under Secretary of Defense for Personnel and Readiness Approval or Senate Confirmation*, DoDI 1320.04, January 3, 2014.

DoD, *DoD Joint Officer Management (JOM) Program*, DoDI 1300.12, March 4, 2014.

DoD, *Inspector General of the Department of Defense (IG DoD)*, DoDD 5106.01, April 20, 2012, Incorporating Change 1, August 19, 2014.

DoD, *Original Appointment of Officers*, DoDI 1310.02, March 26, 2015.

DoD, *Department of Defense Military Equal Opportunity (MEO) Program*, DoDD 1350.2, August 18, 1995, certified current as of November 21, 2003, Incorporating Change 2, June 8, 2015.

DoD, *Initiation of Investigations by Defense Criminal Investigative Organizations*, DoDI 5505.03, March 24, 2011, Incorporating Change 2, February 13, 2017.

DoD, *Procedures for the DoD Personnel Security Program (PSP)*, DoDM 5200.02, April 3, 2017.

DoD, *Investigations by DoD Components*, DoDI 5505.16, June 23, 2017.

DoD, *Inter-Service and Inter-Component Transfers of Service Members*, DoDI 1300.04, July 25, 2017.

DoD, *Harassment Prevention and Response in the Armed Forces*, DoDI 1020.03, February 8, 2018.

DoD, *Titling and Indexing in Criminal Investigations*, DoDI 5505.07, February 28, 2018.

DoD, *Joint Inspectors General Manual*, DoDM 5106.06, May 7, 2018.

DoD, *Diversity Management and Equal Opportunity in the DoD*, DoDD 1020.02E, June 8, 2015, Incorporating Change 2, June 1, 2018.

DoD, *Commissioned Officer Promotion Program Procedures*, DoDI 1320.14, March 13, 2019.

DoD, *Commissioned Officer Administrative Separations*, DoDI 1332.30, May 11, 2018, Incorporating Change 1, April 12, 2019.

Secretary of Defense, "General and Flag Officer Nominations," memorandum for the Secretary of the Army, September 2, 1988.

Secretary of Defense, "Processing Retirement Applications of Officers in the Grades of O-7 and O-8," memorandum for Secretary of the Army; Secretary of the Navy; Secretary of the Air Force; Under Secretary of Defense (Personnel and Readiness); General Counsel, DoD; and Inspector General, DoD, Washington, D.C., October 9, 1998.

Secretary of Defense, "Leading with an Ethics Mindset," memorandum for all Department of Defense personnel, February 2, 2019.

Under Secretary of Defense, "Processing Appointments of Officers Pending Investigation or Adjudication of Adverse Information," memorandum for secretaries of the military departments, January 9, 2015.

Chairman of the Joint Chiefs of Staff

CJCS, *Manpower and Personnel Actions Involving General and Flag Officers*, CJCSI 1331.01D, August 1, 2010, certified current as of February 11, 2013.

CJCS, *Joint Staff Inspector General Responsibilities, Procedures, and Oversight Functions*, CJCSI 5901.01C, November 6, 2015.

CJCS, *Joint Officer Management Program Procedures*, CJCSI 1330.05A, December 12, 2015.

National Guard

Air National Guard, *General Officer Federal Recognition Boards for General Officer Appointment or Promotion in the Air National Guard*, ANGI 36-2501, January 24, 2013.

National Guard Bureau, *Management of the National Guard General Officer Career Management Bench*, CNGBI 0800.01, April 16, 2014.

National Guard Bureau, *Army National Guard Commissioned Officer and Warrant Officer Promotions and Exemplary Conduct Certification Screening (PPOM 17-025)*, ARNG-HRP, April 18, 2017.

National Guard Bureau, *Commissioned Officers Federal Recognition and Related Personnel Actions*, National Guard Regulation 600-100, July 6, 2020.

Army

Army General Officer Management Office, *Senior Leaders Handbook for General Officers*, August 2010.

Department of the Army, *Unfavorable Information*, AR 600-37, December 19, 1986.

Department of the Army, *Equal Employment Opportunity and Affirmative Action*, AR 690-12, March 4, 1988.

Department of the Army, *Unit Equal Opportunity Training Guide*, DA Pamphlet 350-20, June 1, 1994.

Department of the Army, *Military Justice*, AR 27-10, June 24, 1996.

Department of the Army, *Army Grade Determination Review Board and Grade Determinations*, AR 15-80, July 12, 2002.

Department of the Army, *Equal Employment Opportunity Discrimination Complaints*, AR 690-600, February 9, 2004.

Department of the Army, "Policies and Procedures for Reserve Components Officer Selection Boards," DA Memo 600-4, February 9, 2004.

Department of the Army, *Promotion of Commissioned Officers and Warrant Officers Other than General Officers*, AR 135-155, July 13, 2004.

Department of the Army, *Officer Promotions*, AR 600-8-29, February 25, 2005.

Department of the Army, *Officer Transfers and Discharges*, AR 600-8-24, April 12, 2006.

Department of the Army, *Army Command Policy*, AR 600-20, June 7, 2006.

Department of the Army, "Policies and Procedures for Active-Duty List Officer Selection Boards," DA Memo 600-2, September 25, 2006.

Department of the Army, *Procedures for Investigating Officers and Boards of Officers*, AR 15-6, October 2, 2006.

Department of the Army, *Inspector General Activities and Procedures*, AR 20-1, February 1, 2007.

Department of the Army, *Reserve Component General Officer Personnel Management*, AR 135-156, May 17, 2007.

Department of the Army, *Inspector General Activities and Procedures*, AR 20-1, July 3, 2012.

Department of the Army, *Army Military Human Resource Records Management*, AR 600-8-104, April 7, 2014.

Department of the Army, *Army Command Policy*, AR 600-20, November 6, 2014.

Department of the Army, *Procedures for Administrative Investigations and Boards of Officers*, AR 15-6, April 1, 2016.

Department of the Army, *Suspension of Favorable Personnel Actions (Flag)*, AR 600-8-2, May 11, 2016.

Department of the Army, *Equal Employment Opportunity and Diversity*, AR 690-12, December 22, 2016.

Department of the Army, *Separation of Officers*, AR 135-175, November 29, 2017.

Department of the Army, *Unfavorable Information*, AR 600-37, April 10, 2018 (administrative revision, October 1, 2018).

Department of the Army, *Military Human Resources Management*, AR 600-8, July 9, 2019.

Department of the Army Inspector General, *The Assistance and Investigations Guide*, March 2020.

Department of the Army, *Inspector General Activities and Procedures*, AR 20-1, March 23, 2020.

Department of the Army, *Officer Promotions: Personnel—General*, AR 600-8-29, September 9, 2020.

Judge Advocate General's Legal Center and School, U.S. Army, *2015 Commander's Legal Handbook*, Misc. Pub. 27-8, Charlottesville, Va.: Department of the Army, March 2015.

Judge Advocate General's Legal Center and School, U.S. Army, *The U.S. Army Judge Advocate General's School 2017–2018 General Administrative Law Deskbook*, undated.

Secretary of the Army, "Policy Concerning Adverse Information for Officers Being Considered for Promotion, Appointment, or Federal Recognition to a General Officer Grade," memorandum, January 22, 2007.

Secretary of the Army, "Army Directive 2010-10 (Enhancement of the Promotion Review Board Process)," memorandum, December 3, 2010.

Secretary of the Army, "Instructions—Active Component (AC) Promotion Review Board," memorandum for President, promotion review board, April 4, 2016.

Secretary of the Army, "Army Directive 2016-26 (Screening Requirements for Adverse and Reportable Information for Promotion and Federal Recognition to Colonel and Below)," memorandum, July 18, 2016.

Secretary of the Army, "Implementation Guidance for Army Directive 2016-26, Screening Requirements for Adverse and Reportable Information for Promotion and Federal Recognition to Colonel and Below," memorandum for director of military personnel management, February 11, 2019.

Air Force

Air Force General Officer Management Office, *2012 United States Air Force General Officer Handbook*, 2012.

Air National Guard, *General Officer Federal Recognition Boards for General Officer Appointment or Promotion in the Air National Guard*, ANGI 36-2501, January 24, 2013.

Assistant Secretary of the Air Force for Manpower and Reserve Affairs, *Policy Change—Requirement for Commanders to Report Initiation of Commander Directed Investigations (CDI) or Inquiry to the Local IG for All Officers Below the Grade of Brigadier General*, memorandum for all commanders, July 5, 2018.

Department of the Air Force, *Military Equal Opportunity (MEO) Program*, AFI 36-2706, July 29, 2004.

Department of the Air Force, *Equal Employment Opportunity Complaints*, AFI 36-1201, February 12, 2007.

Department of the Air Force, *Inspector General Complaints Resolution*, AFI 90-301, May 15, 2008.

Department of the Air Force, *Officer Promotions and Selective Continuation*, AFI 36-2501, August 17, 2009.

Department of the Air Force, *Equal Opportunity Program, Military and Civilian*, AFI 36-2706, October 5, 2010.

Department of the Air Force, *Unfavorable Information File (UIF) Program*, AFI 36-2907, November 26, 2014.

Department of the Air Force, *Inspector General Complaints Resolution*, AFI 90-301, August 27, 2015.

Department of the Air Force, *Inspector General—The Complaints Resolution Program*, AFPD 90-3, June 9, 2016.

Department of the Air Force, *Service Retirements*, AFI 36-3203, August 30, 2017.

Department of the Air Force, *Inspector General Complaints Resolution*, AFI 90-301, December 28, 2018.

Department of the Air Force, *Air Force Guidance Memorandum to AFI 36-2706, Equal Opportunity Program, Military and Civilian*, AFI 36-2706_AFGM 2017-01, January 28, 2019.

Department of the Air Force, *Equal Opportunity*, AFPD 36-27, March 18, 2019.

Department of the Air Force, *USAF Officer Promotion Review Board (O-6 and Below)*, Air Force Personnel Center Instruction 36-113, July 30, 2019.

Secretary of the Air Force, "SOUIF Decision Policy," memorandum, July 22, 2005.

Secretary of the Air Force, "Air Force Equal Opportunity (EO) and Non-Discrimination Policy Memorandum," May 14, 2014.

Secretary of the Air Force, Office of the Inspector General, Complaints Resolution Directorate, *JAG Guide to IG Investigations*, April 14, 2010.

Secretary of the Air Force, Office of the Inspector General, Complaints Resolution Directorate, *Inspector General Guide for Investigating Officers*, February 2012.

Secretary of the Air Force, Office of the Inspector General, Complaints Resolution Directorate, *Commander Directed Investigation (CDI) Guide*, February 18, 2016.

Navy and Marine Corps

Department of the Navy, *Investigations of Allegations Against Senior Officials of the Department of the Navy*, SECNAVINST 5800.12B, October 18, 2005.

Department of the Navy, *Promotion of Officers to the Grade of Lieutenant (Junior Grade) in the Navy and to the Grade of First Lieutenant in the Marine Corps*, SECNAVINST 1412.6L, December 9, 2005.

Department of the Navy, *Personnel Security Program*, SECNAV M-5510.30, June 2006.

Department of the Navy, *Document Submission Guidelines for the Electronic Military Personnel Records System*, BUPERSINST 1070.27C, November 1, 2010.

Department of the Navy, *Manual of the Judge Advocate General*, JAG Instruction 5800.7F, June 26, 2012.

Department of the Navy, *Administrative Separation of Officers*, SECNAVINST 1920.6C, August 26, 2015.

Department of the Navy, *Navy Equal Opportunity Program Manual*, OPNAVINST 5354.1G, July 24, 2017.

Department of the Navy, *Interservice Transfer of Officers*, SECNAVINST 1000.7G, January 23, 2019.

Department of the Navy, *Department of the Navy Commissioned Officer Promotion Program*, SECNAVINST 1420.3, March 28, 2019.

Department of the Navy, *Promotion of Officers to the Grade of Lieutenant (Junior Grade) in the Navy and to the Grade of First Lieutenant in the Marine Corps*, SECNAVINST 1412.6M, April 15, 2019.

Department of the Navy, *Consideration of Adverse Information by General and Flag Officer Promotion Selection Boards*, SECNAVINST 1401.4B, April 30, 2019.

Department of the Navy, *Selective Retirement, Selective Early Retirement, Selective Early Removal, and Selective Early Discharge of Navy and Marine Corps Commissioned Officers*, SECNAVINST 1920.8, May 20, 2019.

Department of the Navy, *Mission and Functions of the Naval Inspector General*, SECNAVINST 5430.57H, December 17, 2019.

Naval Justice School, *JAGMAN Investigations Handbook*, March 2015.

U.S. Marine Corps, *Law Enforcement Manual*, Marine Corps Order 5580.2B, August 27, 2008.

U.S. Marine Corps, *ODNMS [Officer Disciplinary Notebook Management System] User's Guide*, January 10, 2014.

U.S. Marine Corps, *Marine Corps Prohibited Activities and Conduct Prevention and Response*, Vol. 3, Marine Corps Order 5354.1E, March 26, 2018.

U.S. Marine Corps, *Legal Support and Administration Manual*, Volume 15: *Officer Misconduct and Substandard Performance of Duty*, MCO 5800.16-V15, August 8, 2018.

The U.S. Department of Defense's Adverse and Reportable Information Summary Templates

This appendix presents DoD's templates for adverse and reportable information summaries to be included in officer personnel packages, as of 2019. The template files are titled "O-6 and Below AIS and RIS Sheets" and "O-7 and Above AIS and RIS Sheet Formats," and we found them on the OUSD(P&R) website.[1] The templates are identical for both pay grade groups.

Adverse Information Summary Template

Grade/Name/Service/Component: Grade, Name, Service, Component.

What he or she did: Provide a summary of the incident and a detailed summary of the adverse information. For nominations or appointments as a result of a promotion selection board or Federal recognition board, state whether the adverse information had been reviewed by a promotion selection, Federal Recognition, or promotion review board. If not, state why this information did not meet a board.

Investigating Agency: List any agency that had conducted a review or an investigation into the matter. Include the approval date of the review or investigation and the approval office.

Findings: Provide summary of the findings from the review or investigation. If the official Service position on these findings is different from the review or investigation results, also provide revised findings, who approved, and rationale for revised findings.

Action Taken:

Service: Provide detailed summary of action taken and by whom. If no action was taken, so state and provide rationale why.

OSD: Include the following statement: The Principal Deputy Under Secretary of Defense for Personnel and Readiness (PDUSD (P&R)) and the General Counsel of the Department of Defense (GC, DoD) reviewed the summary of the incident. The PDUSD (P&R) elected to support the nomination; the GC, DoD, asserted no legal objection to the nomination.

---

[1] OUSD(P&R), "OEPM Functions," webpage, undated.

<u>Reasons for Support</u>: State why the Military Department supports the officer for nomination and how the officers meet the requirement of exemplary conduct. State why this nomination or appointment is in the best interest of the Military Department and the Department of Defense. Include comments concerning officer's judgment as it relates to this adverse information. Include any specifics of outstanding items or events from officer's record that counterbalances reported adverse information.

Reportable Information Summary Template

<u>Grade/Name/Service/Component</u>: Grade, Name, Service, Component.

<u>What he or she did</u>: Provide a summary of the incident and a detailed summary of the adverse information.

<u>Investigating Agency</u>: List any agency that had conducted a review or an investigation into the matter. Include the approval date of the review or investigation and the approval office.

<u>Findings</u>: Provide summary of the findings from the review or investigation. If the official Service position on these findings is different from the review or investigation results, also provide revised findings, who approved, and rationale for revised findings.

<u>Action Taken:</u>

<u>Service</u>: Provide detailed summary of action taken and by whom. If no action was taken, so state and provide rationale why.

<u>OSD</u>: Include the following statement: The Principal Deputy Under Secretary of Defense for Personnel and Readiness (PDUSD (P&R)) and the General Counsel of the Department of Defense (GC, DoD) reviewed the summary of the incident. The PDUSD (P&R) elected to support the nomination; the GC, DoD, asserted no legal objection to the nomination.

<u>Reasons for Support</u>: State why the Military Department supports the officer for nomination and how the officer meets the requirement of exemplary conduct. State why this nomination or appointment is in the best interest of the Military Department and the Department of Defense. Include comments concerning officer's judgment as it relates to this adverse information.

<u>Investigating Agency:</u> List any agency that had conducted a review or an investigation into the matter. Include the approval date of the review or investigation and the approval office.

<u>Findings</u>: Provide summary of the findings from the review or investigation. If the official Service position on these findings is different from the review or investigation results, also provide revised findings, who approved, and rationale for revised findings.

<u>Action Taken:</u>

<u>Service</u>: Provide detailed summary of action taken and by whom. If no action was taken, so state and provide rationale why.

<u>OSD</u>: Include the following statement: The Under Secretary of Defense for Personnel and Readiness (USD (P&R)) and the General Counsel of the Department of Defense (GC, DoD) reviewed the summary of the incident. The USD (P&R) elected to support the nomination; the GC, DoD, asserted no legal objection to the nomination.

<u>Reasons for Support</u>: State why the Military Department supports the officer for nomination and how the officer meets the requirement of exemplary conduct. State why this nomination or appointment is in the best interest of the Military Department and the Department of Defense. Include comments concerning officer's judgment as it relates to this adverse information.

References

AFI—*See* Air Force Instruction.

Air Force Instruction 90-301, *Inspector General Complaints Resolution*, Washington, D.C.: Department of the Air Force, December 28, 2018.

Air National Guard Instruction 36-2501, *General Officer Federal Recognition Boards for General Officer Appointment or Promotion in the Air National Guard*, Arlington, Va.: National Guard Bureau, January 24, 2013.

AR—*See* Army Regulation.

Army Inspector General, *The Assistance and Investigations Guide*, Fort Belvoir, Va.: Department of the Army Inspector General Agency Training Division, March 2020.

Army Regulation 15-6, *Procedures for Administrative Investigations and Boards of Officers*, Washington, D.C.: Department of the Army, April 1, 2016.

Army Regulation 20-1, *Inspector General Activities and Procedures*, Washington, D.C.: Department of the Army, March 23, 2020.

Army Regulation 27-10, *Military Justice*, Washington, D.C.: Department of the Army, June 24, 1996.

Assistant Secretary of the Air Force for Manpower and Reserve Affairs, *Policy Change—Requirement for Commanders to Report Initiation of Commander Directed Investigations (CDI) or Inquiry to the Local IG for All Officers Below the Grade of Brigadier General*, memorandum for all commanders, July 5, 2018.

Babcock, Ernest J., *Next Generation Identification (NGI)—Retention and Searching of Noncriminal Justice Fingerprint Submissions*, Washington, D.C.: Federal Bureau of Investigation, February 20, 2015.

Balz, Dan, "Thomas Hearings Resonate Across U.S.: Harassment Controversy Highlights Political, Cultural, Class Divisions," *Washington Post*, October 17, 1991.

Boyd, Aaron, "The Security Clearance Process Is About to Get Its Biggest Overhaul in 50 Years," Nextgov, February 28, 2019.

Browne, Kingsley R., "Military Sex Scandals from Tailhook to the Present: The Cure Can Be Worse Than the Disease," *Duke Journal of Gender Law & Policy*, Vol. 14, 2007, pp. 749–789.

Chairman of the Joint Chiefs of Staff Instruction 1331.01D, *Manpower and Personnel Actions Involving General and Flag Officers*, Washington, D.C.: Joint Chiefs of Staff, August 1, 2010, certified current as of February 11, 2013.

Chambers, William A., Joseph F. Adams, William R. Burns, Jr., Kathleen M. Conley, Rachel D. Dubin, and Waldo D. Freeman, *Review of the Roles, Selection, and Evaluation of Superintendents of Military Service Academies*, Alexandria, Va.: Institute for Defense Analyses, P-5219, December 2014.

Defense Counterintelligence and Security Agency, "History," webpage, undated a. As of March 31, 2020: https://www.dcsa.mil/mc/pv/dod_caf/history/

———, "Self-Report a Security Change or Concern," webpage, undated b. As of April 20, 2020: https://www.dcsa.mil/mc/pv/mbi/self_reporting/

Demirjian, Karoun, "A Colonel Accused a Four-Star General of Sexual Assault. A Senate Panel Will Decide What Happens Next," *Washington Post*, July 28, 2019.

———, "Senate Armed Services Panel Votes to Advance Trump's Pick to Be Military's No. 2, Despite Sexual Assault Allegations," *Washington Post*, July 31, 2019.

Department of Defense Directive 1020.02E, *Diversity Management and Equal Opportunity in the DoD*, Washington, D.C.: U.S. Department of Defense, June 8, 2015, Incorporating Change 2, June 1, 2018.

Department of Defense Directive 1350.2, *Department of Defense Military Equal Opportunity (MEO) Program*, Washington, D.C.: U.S. Department of Defense, August 18, 1995, certified current as of November 21, 2003, Incorporating Change 2, June 8, 2015.

Department of Defense Directive 1440.1, *The DoD Civilian Equal Employment Opportunity (EEO) Program*, Washington, D.C.: U.S. Department of Defense, May 21, 1987, Administrative Reissuance Incorporating Through Change 3, April 17, 1992.

Department of Defense Directive 5106.01, *Inspector General of the Department of Defense*, April 20, 2012, Incorporating Change 1, August 19, 2014.

Department of Defense Directive 5124.8, *Principal Deputy Under Secretary of Defense for Personnel and Readiness (PDUSD(P&R))*, Washington, D.C.: U.S. Department of Defense, July 16, 2003.

Department of Defense Directive 5220.6, *Defense Industrial Personnel Security Clearance Review Program*, Washington, D.C.: U.S. Department of Defense, January 2, 1992, Administrative Reissuance Incorporating Through Change 4, April 20, 1999.

Department of Defense Directive 5500.07-R, *Joint Ethics Regulation (JER)*, Washington, D.C.: U.S. Department of Defense, August 30, 1993, Incorporating Change 7, November 11, 2011.

Department of Defense Directive 5505.06, *Investigations of Allegations of Senior DoD Officials*, Washington, D.C.: U.S. Department of Defense, June 6, 2013.

Department of Defense Instruction 1020.03, *Harassment Prevention and Response in the Armed Forces*, Washington, D.C.: U.S. Department of Defense, February 8, 2018.

Department of Defense Instruction 1300.04, *Inter-Service and Inter-Component Transfers of Service Members*, Washington, D.C.: U.S. Department of Defense, July 25, 2017.

Department of Defense Instruction 1310.02, *Original Appointment of Officers*, Washington, D.C.: U.S. Department of Defense, March 26, 2015.

Department of Defense Instruction 1320.04, *Military Officer Actions Requiring Presidential, Secretary of Defense, or Under Secretary of Defense for Personnel and Readiness Approval or Senate Confirmation*, Washington, D.C.: U.S. Department of Defense, January 3, 2014.

Department of Defense Instruction 1320.4, *Military Officer Actions Requiring Approval of the Secretary of Defense or the President, or Confirmation by the Senate*, Washington, D.C.: U.S. Department of Defense, March 14, 1995.

Department of Defense Instruction 1332.30, *Commissioned Officer Administrative Separations*, Washington, D.C.: U.S. Department of Defense, May 11, 2018, Incorporating Change 1, April 12, 2019.

Department of Defense Instruction 5505.07, *Titling and Indexing in Criminal Investigations*, Washington, D.C.: U.S. Department of Defense, February 28, 2018.

Department of Defense Instruction 5505.16, *Investigations by DoD Components*, Washington, D.C.: U.S. Department of Defense, June 23, 2017.

Department of Defense Manual 5200.02, *Procedures for the DoD Personnel Security Program (PSP)*, Washington, D.C.: U.S. Department of Defense, April 3, 2017.

Department of Defense Manual 6025.13, *Medical Quality Assurance (MQA) and Clinical Quality Management in the Military Health Care System (MHS)*, Washington, D.C.: U.S. Department of Defense, October 29, 2013.

District of Columbia v. Wesby, 138 S. Ct. 577, 2018.

DoD—*See* U.S. Department of Defense.

DoDD—*See* Department of Defense Directive.

DoDI—*See* Department of Defense Instruction.

DoD OIG—*See* U.S. Department of Defense Office of Inspector General.

Edmond v. United States, 520 U.S. 651, 1997.

EEOC—*See* U.S. Equal Employment Opportunity Commission.

EEOC OIG—*See* Equal Employment Opportunity Commission Office of the Inspector General.

Equal Employment Opportunity Commission Office of the Inspector General, *Draft Report: Evaluation of EEOC Federal Hearings and Appeals Processes*, OIG Report No. 2018-01-EOIG, March 27, 2020.

Esper, Mark T., "Immediate Actions to Address Diversity, Inclusion, and Equal Opportunity in the Military Services," memorandum for Chief Management Officer of the Department of Defense et al., Washington, D.C.: U.S. Department of Defense, July 14, 2020.

FBI—*See* Federal Bureau of Investigation.

Federal Bureau of Investigation, "National Crime Information Center (NCIC)," webpage, undated a. As of March 29, 2020:
https://www.fbi.gov/services/cjis/ncic

———, "Next Generation Identification (NGI)," webpage, undated b. As of March 31, 2020:
https://www.fbi.gov/services/cjis/fingerprints-and-other-biometrics/ngi

Figinski, Theodore F., "The Effect of Potential Activations on the Employment of Military Reservists: Evidence from a Field Experiment," *ILR Review*, Vol. 70, No. 4, August 2017, pp. 1037–1056.

Fine, Glenn A., "Senior Leader Misconduct: Prevention and Accountability," statement presented before the Subcommittee on Military Personnel, House Armed Services Committee, U.S. House of Representatives, Washington, D.C., February 7, 2018.

FY 2019 National Defense Authorization Act—*See* Public Law 115-232.

FY 2020 National Defense Authorization Act—*See* Public Law 116-92.

FY 2021 National Defense Authorization Act—*See* Public Law 116-283.

"Glenn Defense Marine Asia and the US 7th Fleet (the 'Fat Leonard' Scandal)," *Compendium of Arms Trade Corruption*, webpage, last updated June 9, 2020. As of September 11, 2020:
https://sites.tufts.edu/corruptarmsdeals/glenn-defense-marine-asia-and-the-us-7th-fleet-the-fat-leonard-scandal/

Harrell, Margaret C., and William M. Hix, *Managing Adverse and Reportable Information Regarding General and Flag Officers*, Santa Monica, Calif.: RAND Corporation, MG-1088-OSD, 2012. As of September 9, 2020:
https://www.rand.org/pubs/monographs/MG1088.html

Harvard Law School, "Congressional Restrictions on the President's Appointment Power and the Role of Longstanding Practice in Constitutional Interpretation," *Harvard Law Review*, Vol. 120, No. 7, May 2007, pp. 1914–1917.

Illinois v. Gates, 462 U.S. 213, 243–244, 1983.

JAGINST—*See* JAG Instruction.

JAG Instruction 5800.7F, *Manual of the Judge Advocate General*, Washington, D.C.: Department of the Navy, June 26, 2012.

Kamarck, Kristy N., *Military Retirement: Background and Recent Developments*, Washington, D.C.: Congressional Research Service, RL34751, last updated July 12, 2019.

Kheel, Rebecca, "Gillibrand Tears into Army Nominee over Military Sexual Assault: 'You're Failing Us,'" *The Hill*, May 2, 2019.

Lamothe, Dan, "Exclusive: Nuke Cheating Scandal Puts Promotions for Air Force Brass on Ice," *Foreign Policy*, January 30, 2014.

Leone, Carman A., "Ordered to Self-Incriminate: The Unconstitutionality of Self-Report Policies in the Armed Forces," *Air Force Law Review*, Vol. 78, 2018, pp. 125–168.

Madison, James, *The Debates in the Federal Convention of 1787 Which Framed the Constitution of the United States of America*, eds. Gaillard Hunt and James Brown Scott, New York: Oxford University Press, [1787] 1920.

Marine Corps Order 5800.16-V15, *Legal Support and Administration Manual*, Washington, D.C.: Marine Corps, August 8, 2018.

Marquis, Jefferson P., Coreen Farris, Kimberly Curry Hall, Kristy N. Kamarck, Nelson Lim, Douglas Shontz, Paul S. Steinberg, Robert Stewart, Thomas E. Trail, Jennie W. Wenger, Anny Wong, and Eunice C. Wong, *Improving Oversight and Coordination of Department of Defense Programs That Address Problematic Behaviors Among Military Personnel*, Santa Monica, Calif.: RAND Corporation, RR-1352-OSD, 2017. As of September 9, 2020:
https://www.rand.org/pubs/research_reports/RR1352.html

Mascott, Jennifer L., "Who Are 'Officers of the United States'?" *Stanford Law Review*, Vol. 70, No. 2, February 2018, p. 443–564.

Matthews, Miriam, and Nelson Lim, *Improving the Timeliness of Equal Employment Opportunity Complaint Processing in Department of Defense*, Santa Monica, Calif.: RAND Corporation, RR-680-OSD, 2015. As of September 9, 2020:
https://www.rand.org/pubs/research_reports/RR680.html

MCO—*See* Marine Corps Order.

Military Rules of Evidence, Section III, Exclusionary Rules and Related Matters Concerning Self-Incrimination, Search and Seizure, and Eyewitness Identification; Rule 315, Probable Cause Searches, June 2015. As of May 21, 2021:
https://www.federalregister.gov/documents/2015/06/22/2015-15495/
2015-amendments-to-the-manual-for-courts-martial-united-states

Myers, Meghann, "Gillibrand Grills Next Army Chief on Rise of Sexual Assaults, Decrease in Prosecutions," *Army Times*, May 2, 2019.

Narain, Balaji L., and Dustin Banks, "Administrative Investigations and Non-Judicial Punishment in Joint Environments," *The Reporter*, May 23, 2019.

National Guard, "Inspector General (NGB-IG)," webpage, undated. As of May 15, 2020:
https://www.nationalguard.mil/Leadership/Joint-Staff/Personal-Staff/Inspector-General/

National Guard Regulation 600-100, *Commissioned Officers Federal Recognition and Related Personnel Actions*, Arlington, Va.: National Guard Bureau, July 6, 2020.

Office of the Deputy Assistant Secretary of Defense for Military Community and Family Policy, *2018 Demographics: Profile of the Military Community*, Washington, D.C.: U.S. Department of Defense, 2019. As of September 9, 2020:
https://download.militaryonesource.mil/12038/MOS/Reports/2018-demographics-report.pdf

Office of the Inspector General of the Department of Defense, *Review of DoD-Directed Investigations of Detainee Abuse (U)*, Arlington, Va., Report No. 06-INTEL-10, August 25, 2006a.

———, "Review of DoD-Directed Investigations of Detainee Abuse (U) (Redacted)," webpage, August 25, 2006b. As of September 10, 2020:
https://www.dodig.mil/reports.html/Article/1142215/
review-of-dod-directed-investigations-of-detainee-abuse-classified/

Office of the Under Secretary of Defense for Personnel and Readiness, "OEPM Functions," webpage, undated. As of December 9, 2019:
https://prhome.defense.gov/M-RA/_ARCHIVE-2018/MPP/OEPM/Functions/

———, "Memorandum Provides Instructions for the Processing of Three- and Four-Star Retirement Recommendations," memorandum for Secretary of the Army, Secretary of the Navy, Secretary of the Air Force, and Chairman of the Joint Chiefs of Staff, Washington, D.C., June 21, 1996.

OUSD(P&R)—*See* Office of the Under Secretary of Defense for Personnel and Readiness.

Public Law 92-544, An Act Making Appropriations for the Departments of State, Justice, and Commerce, the Judiciary, and Related Agencies for the Fiscal Year Ending June 30, 1973, and for Other Purposes, October 25, 1972. As of July 31, 2021:
https://www.govinfo.gov/content/pkg/STATUTE-86/pdf/STATUTE-86-Pg1109.pdf

Public Law 109-163, National Defense Authorization Act for Fiscal Year 2006, January 6, 2006. As of September 9, 2020:
https://www.govinfo.gov/app/details/PLAW-109publ163

Public Law 115-232, John S. McCain National Defense Authorization Act for Fiscal Year 2019, August 13, 2018. As of September 9, 2020:
https://www.govinfo.gov/app/details/PLAW-115publ232

Public Law 116-92, National Defense Authorization Act for Fiscal Year 2020, December 20, 2019. As of September 9, 2021:
https://www.congress.gov/116/plaws/publ92/PLAW-116publ92.pdf

Public Law 116-283, William M. [Mac] Thornberry National Defense Authorization Act for Fiscal Year 2021, January 1, 2021. As of September 15, 2021:
https://www.congress.gov/bill/116th-congress/house-bill/6395/text

Scarborough, Rowan, "10,000 Navy Jobs Cut: The Reason—Tailhook or Politics?" *Washington Times*, June 30, 1992.

———, "Navy Chief Reverses: Won't Promote Pilot Cleared in Tailhook," *Washington Times*, December 29, 1995.

———, "Tailhook Officer Gives Up Fight for Promotion, Retires: Navy Officials Relieved That Battle Is Over," *Washington Times*, July 13, 1996a.

———, "Lawmakers Ease Tailhook Promotions: Panel Also Orders Process to Help Officers Answer Charges," *Washington Times*, September 28, 1996b.

Secretary of Defense, "General and Flag Officer Nominations," memorandum for the Secretary of the Army, Washington, D.C., September 2, 1988a.

———, "Processing Retirement Applications of Officers in the Grades of O-7 and O-8," memorandum for Secretary of the Army; Secretary of the Navy; Secretary of the Air Force; Under Secretary of Defense (Personnel and Readiness); General Counsel, DoD; and Inspector General, DoD, Washington, D.C., October 9, 1998b.

———, "Leading with an Ethics Mindset," memorandum for all Department of Defense personnel, February 2, 2019.

Under Secretary of Defense, "Processing Appointments of Officers Pending Investigation or Adjudication of Adverse Information," memorandum for secretaries of the military departments, January 9, 2015.

United States v. Serianne, 69 M.J. 8, 9, C.A.A.F., 2010.

U.S. Code, Title 5, Government Organization and Employees; Title 5, Appendix. As of September 14, 2020:
https://www.govinfo.gov/app/details/USCODE-2011-title5/USCODE-2011-title5-app/summary

———, Title 10, Armed Forces; Subtitle A, General Military Law; Part I, Organization and General Military Powers; Chapter 2, Department of Defense; Section 113, Secretary of Defense. As of September 14, 2020:
https://www.govinfo.gov/app/details/USCODE-2011-title10/
USCODE-2011-title10-subtitleA-partI-chap2-sec113

———, Title 10, Armed Forces; Subtitle A, General Military Law; Part I, Organization and General Military Powers; Chapter 4, Office of the Secretary of Defense; Section 141, Inspector General. As of September 14, 2020:
https://www.govinfo.gov/app/details/USCODE-2011-title10/
USCODE-2011-title10-subtitleA-partI-chap4-sec141

————, Title 10, Armed Forces; Subtitle A, General Military Law; Part II, Personnel; Chapter 33, Original Appointments of Regular Officers in Grades Above Warrant Officer Grades; Section 531, Original Appointments of Commissioned Officers. As of September 10, 2020:
https://www.govinfo.gov/app/details/USCODE-2011-title10/
USCODE-2011-title10-subtitleA-partII-chap33-sec531

————, Title 10, Armed Forces; Subtitle A, General Military Law; Part II, Personnel; Chapter 33, Original Appointments of Regular Officers in Grades Above Warrant Officer Grades; Section 532, Qualifications for Original Appointment as a Commissioned Officer. As of September 10, 2020:
https://www.govinfo.gov/app/details/USCODE-2010-title10/
USCODE-2010-title10-subtitleA-partII-chap33-sec532

————, Title 10, Armed Forces; Subtitle A, General Military Law; Part II, Personnel; Chapter 36, Promotion, Separation, and Involuntary Retirement of Officers on the Active-Duty List; Subchapter I, Selection Boards. As of September 10, 2020:
https://www.govinfo.gov/app/details/USCODE-2011-title10/USCODE-2011-title10-subtitleA-partII-chap36

————, Title 10, Armed Forces; Subtitle A, General Military Law; Part II, Personnel; Chapter 36, Promotion, Separation, and Involuntary Retirement of Officers on the Active-Duty List; Subchapter II, Promotions; Section 624, Promotions: How Made. As of September 10, 2020:
https://www.govinfo.gov/app/details/USCODE-1996-title10/
USCODE-1996-title10-subtitleA-partII-chap36-subchapII-sec624

————, Title 10, Armed Forces; Subtitle A, General Military Law; Part II, Personnel; Chapter 36, Promotion, Separation, and Involuntary Retirement of Officers on the Active-Duty List; Subchapter III, Failure of Selection for Promotion and Retirement for Years of Service; Section 628, Special Selection Boards. As of September 10, 2020:
https://www.govinfo.gov/app/details/USCODE-2011-title10/
USCODE-2011-title10-subtitleA-partII-chap36-subchapIII-sec628

————, Title 10, Armed Forces; Subtitle A, General Military Law; Part II, Personnel; Chapter 36, Promotion, Separation, and Involuntary Retirement of Officers on the Active-Duty List; Subchapter III, Failure of Selection for Promotion and Retirement for Years of Service; Section 629, Removal from a List of Officers Recommended for Promotion. As of September 10, 2020:
https://www.govinfo.gov/app/details/USCODE-2010-title10/
USCODE-2010-title10-subtitleA-partII-chap36-subchapIII-sec629

————, Title 10, Armed Forces; Subtitle A, General Military Law; Part II, Personnel; Chapter 47, Uniform Code of Military Justice; Subchapter III, Non-Judicial Punishment; Section 815, Article 15, Commanding Officer's Non-Judicial Punishment. As of September 14, 2020:
https://www.govinfo.gov/app/details/USCODE-2010-title10/
USCODE-2010-title10-subtitleA-partII-chap47-subchapIII-sec815

————, Title 10, Armed Forces; Subtitle A, General Military Law; Part II, Personnel; Chapter 69, Retired Grade; Section 1370, Commissioned Officers: General Rule; Exceptions. As of September 10, 2020:
https://www.govinfo.gov/app/details/USCODE-2010-title10/
USCODE-2010-title10-subtitleA-partII-chap69-sec1370

————, Title 10, Armed Forces; Subtitle A, General Military Law; Part II, Personnel; Chapter 71, Computation of Retired Pay. As of September 10, 2020:
https://www.govinfo.gov/app/details/USCODE-2010-title10/USCODE-2010-title10-subtitleA-partII-chap71

————, Title 10, Armed Forces; Subtitle B, Army; Part II, Personnel; Chapter 725, Rank and Command; Section 7233, Requirement of Exemplary Conduct. As of March 10, 2021:
https://www.govinfo.gov/app/details/USCODE-2018-title10/USCODE-2018-title10-subtitleB-partII-chap725-sec7233

————, Title 10, Armed Forces; Subtitle C, Navy and Marine Corps; Part II, Personnel; Chapter 821, Officers in Command; Section 8167, Requirement of Exemplary Conduct. As of March 10, 2021:
https://www.govinfo.gov/app/details/USCODE-2018-title10/
USCODE-2018-title10-subtitleC-partII-chap821-sec8167

———, Title 10, Armed Forces; Subtitle D, Air Force; Part II, Personnel; Chapter 925, Rank and Command; Section 9233, Requirement of Exemplary Conduct. As of March 10, 2021:
https://www.govinfo.gov/app/details/USCODE-2018-title10/
USCODE-2018-title10-subtitleD-partII-chap925-sec9233

———, Title 10, Armed Forces; Subtitle E, Reserve Components; Part I, Organization and Administration; Chapter 1007, Administration of Reserve Components; Section 10216, Military Technicians (Dual Status). As of September 10, 2020:
https://www.govinfo.gov/app/details/USCODE-2009-title10/
USCODE-2009-title10-subtitleE-partI-chap1007-sec10216

———, Title 10, Armed Forces; Subtitle E, Reserve Components; Part II, Personnel Generally; Chapter 1205, Appointment of Reserve Officers; Section 12211, Officers: Army National Guard of the United States. As of August 1, 2021:
https://www.govinfo.gov/app/details/USCODE-2011-title10/USCODE-2011-title10-subtitleE-partII-chap1205-sec12211

———, Title 10, Armed Forces; Subtitle E, Reserve Components; Part II, Personnel Generally; Chapter 1205, Appointment of Reserve Officers; Section 12212, Officers: Air National Guard of the United States. As of August 1, 2021:
https://www.govinfo.gov/app/details/USCODE-2015-title10/USCODE-2015-title10-subtitleE-partII-chap1205-sec12212

———, Title 10, Armed Forces; Subtitle E, Reserve Components; Part II, Personnel Generally; Chapter 1205, Appointment of Reserve Officers; Section 12203, Commissioned Officers: Appointment, How Made; Term. As of September 10, 2020:
https://www.govinfo.gov/app/details/USCODE-2010-title10/
USCODE-2010-title10-subtitleE-partII-chap1205-sec12203

———, Title 10, Armed Forces; Subtitle E, Reserve Components; Part III, Promotion and Retention of Officers on the Reserve Active-Status List; Chapter 1403, Selection Boards; Section 14107, Information Furnished by the Secretary Concerned to Promotion Boards. As of September 14, 2020:
https://www.govinfo.gov/app/details/USCODE-2009-title10/
USCODE-2009-title10-subtitleE-partIII-chap1403-sec14107

———, Title 10, Armed Forces; Subtitle E, Reserve Components; Part III, Promotion and Retention of Officers on the Reserve Active-Status List; Chapter 1403, Selection Boards; Section 14108, Recommendations by Promotion Boards. As of August 1, 2021:
https://www.govinfo.gov/app/details/USCODE-2020-title10/
USCODE-2020-title10-subtitleE-partIII-chap1403-sec14108

———, Title 10, Armed Forces; Subtitle E, Reserve Components; Part III, Promotion and Retention of Officers on the Reserve Active-Status List; Chapter 1405, Promotions; Section 14311, Delay of Promotion: Involuntary. As of September 10, 2020:
https://www.govinfo.gov/app/details/USCODE-2011-title10/
USCODE-2011-title10-subtitleE-partIII-chap1405-sec14311

———, Title 10, Armed Forces; Subtitle E, Reserve Components; Part III, Promotion and Retention of Officers on the Reserve Active-Status List; Chapter 1407, Failure of Selection for Promotion and Involuntary Separation; Section 14502, Special Selection Boards: Correction of Errors. As of August 1, 2021:
https://www.govinfo.gov/app/details/USCODE-2011-title10/USCODE-2011-title10-subtitleE-partIII-chap1407-sec14502

———, Title 32, National Guard; Chapter 3, Personnel; Section 307, Federal Recognition of Officers: Examination; Certificate of Eligibility. As of September 10, 2020:
https://www.govinfo.gov/app/details/USCODE-2011-title32/USCODE-2011-title32-chap3-sec307

———, Title 34, Crime Control and Law Enforcement; Subtitle IV, Criminal Records and Information; Chapter 403, Criminal Justice Identification, Information, and Communication; Subchapter II, Exchange of Criminal History Records for Noncriminal Justice Purposes. As of September 14, 2020:
https://www.govinfo.gov/content/pkg/USCODE-2018-title34/pdf/
USCODE-2018-title34-subtitleIV-chap403-subchapII.pdf

U.S. Constitution, Philadelphia, Pa., 1788.

U.S. Department of Defense, *Manual for Courts-Martial United States (2019 Edition)*, Washington, D.C., 2019.

U.S. Department of Defense Office of Inspector General, "Our Mission," webpage, undated. As of September 14, 2020:
https://www.dodig.mil/About/Mission/

―――, *Task Force to Improve Timeliness of Senior Officer Administrative Investigations (Redacted)*, Alexandria, Va.: U.S. Department of Defense, DoDIG-2015-030, November 4, 2014. As of September 9, 2020:
https://www.dodig.mil/Reports/Administrative-Investigations/Article/1119093/
task-force-to-improve-timeliness-of-senior-official-administrative-investigatio/

―――, *Semiannual Report to the Congress*, Alexandria, Va.: U.S. Department of Defense, October 1, 2019–March 31, 2020. As of May 25, 2021:
https://media.defense.gov/2020/Jul/30/2002467835/-1/-1/1/
SAR_MAR_2020_BOOK%20V5%20SIGNED_FINAL_20200730_508.PDF

U.S. Department of Labor, "Equal Employment Opportunity," webpage, undated. As of July 18, 2020:
https://www.dol.gov/general/topic/discrimination

U.S. Government Accountability Office, *Military Personnel: Factors Affecting Approval Time for Officer Appointments*, Washington, D.C., GAO-19-527R, June 27, 2019.

U.S. Equal Employment Opportunity Commission, "Overview of Federal Sector EEO Complaint Process," webpage, undated. As of May 10, 2020:
https://www.eeoc.gov/federal-sector/overview-federal-sector-eeo-complaint-process

―――, "Performance and Accountability Report Fiscal Year 2018," webpage, November 15, 2018. As of September 14, 2020:
https://www.eeoc.gov/performance-and-accountability-report-fiscal-year-2018

U.S. Government Accountability Office, *Military Personnel: Factors Affecting Approval Time for Officer Appointments*, Washington, D.C., GAO-19-527R, June 27, 2019.

U.S. Office of Personnel Management, *Completing Your Investigation Request in e-QIP: Guide for the Standard Form (SF) 86*, Washington, D.C., July 2018. As of September 14, 2020:
https://www.dcsa.mil/Portals/91/Documents/pv/mbi/standard-form-sf-86-guide-for-applicants.pdf

U.S. Senate, "Nominations: A Historical Overview," webpage, undated. As of October 14, 2019:
https://www.senate.gov/artandhistory/history/common/briefing/Nominations.htm

U.S. Senate Committee on Armed Services, "History," webpage, undated a. As of April 30, 2020:
https://www.armed-services.senate.gov/about/history

―――, "Nominations," webpage, undated b. As of April 30, 2020:
https://www.armed-services.senate.gov/nominations

―――, "Rules of Procedure," webpage, undated c. As of April 30, 2020:
https://www.armed-services.senate.gov/about/rules

U.S. Statutes at Large, 1st Congress, 2nd session, Statute II, Chapter 9, An Act for the Punishment of Certain Crimes Against the United States, April 30, 1790.

Weiss v. United States, 510 U.S. 163, 1994.

Werner, Ben, "Navy Stopped Publicly Announcing Flag Officer Nominations, Citing Policy Review," USNI News, last updated February 28, 2019.